FLOWERS – CUT AND DRIED

FLOWERS

CUT

AND

DRIED

THE ESSENTIAL
GUIDE TO
GROWING, DRYING
AND ARRANGING

CAROLINE
ALEXANDER

WITH PHOTOGRAPHY
BY SARA TAYLOR

KYLE CATHIE LIMITED

First published in Great Britain in 1999 by
Kyle Cathie Limited
20 Vauxhall Bridge Road
London SW1V 2SA

10 9 8 7 6 5 4 3 2 1

ISBN 1 85626 289 8

Editor: Sophie Bessemer
Copy-editor: Heather Dewhurst
Designer: Geoff Hayes
Stylist: Wei Tang
Indexer: Valerie Chandler
Production: Lorraine Baird

A Cataloguing in Publications record for this title is
available from the British Library.

Colour separations by Colourpath Ltd
Printed and bound in Singapore by KHL Printing Co.Pte. Ltd.

Dedication

This book is dedicated to my husband
William, my children Lorna, Thomas
and Crispin, and to my parents.

CONTENTS

INTRODUCTION

introduction

The art of drying flowers has been with us for centuries but the art of designing with dried flowers is excitingly new. In the past flowers were cut and dried for their medicinal or culinary qualities and it tended not to matter what they looked like. But recently there has been a revolution – technology has allowed all manner of plant material to be preserved with a level of quality and colour retention hitherto undreamed of, and international trading has made available varieties from all over the world. There is a feast of possibilities awaiting anyone who enjoys working with flowers.

You don't need to be a horticulturist to grow flowers for drying, you don't need high-tech equipment to dry them and you certainly don't need to be a trained florist to arrange them. You just need to understand them and to like their colours, shapes and textures. Learning about them is a voyage of discovery – and one that I embarked on myself about twelve years ago. The fascination still has not waned and the more I get to know them, the more I delight in their versatility.

Flowers – Cut and Dried is the culmination of those years of experimentation, of growing, harvesting, drying and arranging. Working on the family farm, and developing a specialist business with dried flowers, I have experienced the disappointment of bad weather spoiling a crop, and have learnt the hard way that glorious blooms can lose their petals if picked too late, but, I have also had the pleasure of creating displays that have lasted for months and the thrill of them being mistaken for fresh flowers because of their colour.

The realisation that my approach to the flowers was so radically different to that of many other people gave rise to the desire to write a book that challenged the conventional view. I wanted to rectify some common misconceptions about 'everlasting flowers', to give a real understanding of the critical factors that affected quality, to explain how to create successful displays (a very different process to arranging fresh flowers) and especially to illustrate the vibrancy of colour that could be achieved.

To be worthwhile, the book needed to be comprehensive – a definitive guide to dried flowers – so it starts with the place of dried flowers in history (an apt reminder that the flowers have many qualities to commend them other than their looks) before tracing the development of modern drying methods.

The key to successful growing and drying of flowers, whether commercially or at home, is to be able to predict the exact stage at which they should be harvested and to select the right method and speed of drying. To do this, you need to know what particular characteristic of the plant you want to retain and to predict how the plant's form will change during the drying process. It sounds complicated but it isn't. The book's approach, to make it simple, is to group the plants according to the stage of development at which they are harvested – in bud, early flower, full flower, seed-pod and so on. Once grasped, these principles can easily be applied to other varieties in the garden and other methods of drying and the possibilities are then endless.

In books on flowers there is always the dilemma as to whether to refer to them by their Latin or common names. What I have chosen to do here is to select whichever name is most frequently used within the flower trade. For instance, safflower is invariably referred to as *Carthamus* whereas cornflower is always cornflower, not *Centaurea cyanus*; *Limonium dumosum* is generally referred to as sea lavender but within the trade is known as 'Dumosa' so you will find this term too. At first this mixture may seem confusing but will, I assure you, become easier with familiarity. The index and the directory format of the chapter on growing flowers at home (pages 30 to 81) will also help

Once the foundations have been laid for design work – highlighting important considerations like location, light and humidity – I have concentrated on the crucial topics of how to select the right varieties to blend with one another and, particularly important in the case of dried flowers, how to co-ordinate floral themes to interior decor. (Because dried flowers last a long time they are invariably required to link to a colour scheme.) Advising on colour is always tricky because of personal likes and dislikes but there are ground-rules which anyone can follow with success.

Developing an eye for colour, balance and harmony is important. My own approach to arranging the flowers has always been based on such instincts and my methods are similar to those of an artist. The process of putting together a display – the art of dried flowers – has therefore been described in the terminology of painting or sculpture.

Displaying varieties together as vibrantly and boldly as possible establishes a strong visual impact which lasts a long time, but dried flowers also lend themselves to great subtlety. The designs which include a fabric back-drop, especially the terracotta vase of sunflowers on page 41 and the Chinese vase in blue and white on page 129, were particularly satisfying to create because they show the flowers as set pieces – works of art in their own right, worthy of being given a special place in a room.

All the photographs – and even the projects in the final chapter – are there to give inspiration rather than to be copied. It is much more satisfying to create something of your own and I hope that this book provides the insight and the understanding to enable that to happen.

The process of writing a book requires a considerable expenditure of time and effort. The investment is justified when the content of the book says something different from what has been said before and can provide new knowledge, inspiration and food for thought. *Flowers – Cut and Dried* is entirely personal in its viewpoint but has, I trust, the credibility of experience – many years growing, drying and designing with dried flowers at The Hop Shop, as well as five Gold Medals at the RHS Chelsea Flower Show. I hope now that this book has relevance to all who love flowers and justifies the faith of my publishers in waiting several years for me to put my thoughts on paper!

Caroline Alexander

DRIED
FLOWERS
IN
HISTORY

flowers in ancient times

There has always been a fascination with 'everlasting' flowers – the 'immortelles' – that can retain their beauty and character long after the living sap has drained from them. Fresh flowers may owe much of their charm to their innate transience, but it is dried flowers that appeal to that part of human nature that has always desired to preserve beauty and achieve immortality. It is not surprising, therefore, that the practice of preserving flowers is an ancient tradition which has just as much relevance to today's society as it did to the Ancient Greeks.

Today, the art of drying flowers is primarily for decorative use. Because of consumer demand, coupled with new technological developments, the skill extends well beyond the traditional 'everlastings' to a spectacular range of species whose natural lives as objects of beauty can be lengthened by an assortment of methods – air-drying, pressing, freeze-drying, preserving, glycerining and silica-drying! However, many of the varieties that are now popular have long been a familiar part of old customs and traditions. Their contribution to our cultural history was not only the result of their medicinal, functional or culinary values, but because of the spiritual powers that were attributed to, or associated with, them.

There is evidence, dating back thousands of years, of flowers being used in burial rituals or made into crowns to denote rank or status. Some flowers adorning the coffins of ancient Egyptian kings may have been chosen for their medicinal or aromatic qualities but others were undoubtedly selected to symbolize immortality, such as certain varieties of *Helichrysum* and *Delphinium*. It is said that the flower petals still retained their colour when the tombs were opened thousands of years later.

◼ MYTHOLOGY AND IMMORTALITY

Immortality was a popular theme in the legends of the Ancient Greeks and the myths contain frequent references to flowers in connection with gods and heroes – hence *Hyacinth, Narcissus* and *Achillea*. Particular everlasting varieties were associated with remembrance and used as funeral tokens. The name *Amaranthus*, when translated, means 'not wither', and the globe amaranth (*Gomphrena globosa*) was used to honour the dead, being woven into garlands or strewn on floors. *Achillea millefolium*, common yarrow, was reputedly used by Achilles to heal his soldiers' battle wounds; in medieval Europe it was later known as Knights' Milfoil and valued for the same purpose.

◼ CLASSICAL ASSOCIATIONS

The reverence with which flowers were regarded in Greek culture also influenced the Romans and it became customary for status to be denoted by a strict code of flower symbolism. In addition to the

Engraving showing Achilles healing Telephus, from which act the healing plant we know as yarrow was given the name Achillea.

well-known laurel wreaths, which were awarded like medals, there were other symbolic crowns including *Hibernae coronae*, made from dried flowers and herbs. Bridal crowns incorporated the wild marjoram – *Origanum vulgare* – as well as other sweet-smelling herbs, such as *Solidago*, whose name means 'to join'.

flowers in medieval times

MEDIEVAL SYMBOLISM

The symbolism of certain plant varieties was carried over from Greek and Roman customs into early Christian beliefs. For instance, the lily embodied the purity of the Virgin Mary, and the long-lasting amaranths were associated with the resurrection and immortality of Christ. The lavish use of flowers in rituals and festivities was discouraged by the early church as having too many pagan associations but the functional attributes of plants were exploited to the full.

THE MONASTERY GARDEN

Many plants would still have been collected from the wild but the monasteries of medieval Europe created some of the earliest gardens that combined food production with the growing of medicinal plants, and we know that the monks had all the necessary expertise for harvesting, distilling, drying or processing their crops. The monks also established the garden as a place of relaxation and contemplation of nature's beauty – a place where plants could be enjoyed for their ornamental value and their ability to uplift the spirits.

PRACTICAL USES OF FLOWERS

In those days of self-sufficiency no plant was neglected if it could be used to serve a purpose – as a food, as a herbal or spicy flavouring, for dyeing, for construction, for making utensils, rope or roofing materials, for weaving fabric, for its

(above) Medieval depiction of sage being picked.

(following pages) Collections of herbs, tied with raffia or string and informally arranged, can capture the mood of times past. Here are hops, thyme, sage, heads of Allium, Solidago *and marjoram as well as tansy, bay leaves and trailing* Amaranthus.

The Apothecary's Rose –
Rosa gallica officinalis. *The*
perfume of its dried petals
has been prized for many
centuries.

aroma, as an insect repellent or medicine – and a complex folklore developed regarding herbal cures for all manner of ailments. Drying and preserving were crucial skills that were part of a woman's housework, with tips and recipes being passed down the generations. These recipes were not only for food and medicines but also for inks and cloth dyes. For instance, the herb marjoram was used as the basis for a purple dye, the safflower (*Carthamus tinctorius*) for red, and the valuable saffron from the crocus for yellow.

INSECT REPELLENTS

Before the introduction of commercial food production and refrigerated storage, it was essential to the survival of the household that grain, fruit and other foodstuffs harvested in the summer could be effectively preserved and stored for consumption during the winter. Keeping vermin out was a constant problem (a job given to dogs before the introduction of cats as household pets), but mould and insects were equally as damaging. Certain items could be safeguarded by hanging them to dry from beams or rafters and those plants which had useful insect-repelling properties, such as rosemary, lavender, *Santolina*, feverfew and tansy, would have been hung alongside them. These were used to deter not only flies but troublesome moths, fleas and bed-bugs as well.

We can be certain therefore that the habit of hanging flowers to dry in the house is not just a modern fashion but a time-honoured tradition.

MEDICINAL USES OF FLOWERS

Many medicinal plants would have needed to be processed fresh to obtain the maximum benefit from their oils, but culinary herbs such as thyme, savory, sage and marjoram, would have been cut in the summer, hung and left to dry until required many months later.

Of the culinary herbs, sage and thyme were also valued for their antiseptic and anti-fungal powers. When used as a stuffing in meat, sage helped destroy bacteria and so reduced the likelihood of food poisoning in the days when meat would have been well-hung before consumption. Apart from their skin-healing properties, dried marigold petals were used to decorate and flavour winter stews, rubbed into cheese to improve its colour, and mixed with sugar to make conserve.

AROMATIC USES OF FLOWERS

Rushes were strewn on the floors of medieval buildings to act as disposable carpets, absorbing spillages and providing some insulation. Herbs like meadowsweet, thyme, rosemary and hyssop (which releases an orangey smell) were added for their scent which intensifies when crushed underfoot. Such locally gathered flowers were strewn in churches on festive or wedding days. One partic-ularly popular herb in Europe was woodruff which contains coumarin. Its scent, which is like new-mown hay, was released as it dried, so it acted like a room freshener, much appreciated in the days when standards of hygiene left a lot to be desired!

The Apothecary's Rose, *Rosa gallica officinalis*, was renowned for its perfume. The petals were dried and powdered, or scattered among stored clothes. Rosewater was made as a tonic or skin cleanser and rose oil used as a scent.

Of the aromatic plants, lavender was then, as now, one of the most popular and versatile, its oil having antiseptic and soothing qualities and its flowers being used to scent linen as well as being an effective deterrent against moths and mice.

FLOWERS IN INTERIORS

There is little evidence of cut flowers being used for everyday decoration in the home. In medieval times, the number of household effects that ordinary people owned were limited. Furniture and furnishings tended to be functional and decorative ornaments were only for the wealthy. Glass was scarce and ceramics expensive. Even though there would have been water-holding containers – metal drinking vessels and jugs, leather buckets, wooden barrels and glazed pottery – it is unlikely that many would have been considered appropriate for displaying fresh flowers and there were certainly not many surfaces on which to display them or any good lighting to view them. Most flowers brought into the home would have been hung to dry and we can only speculate as to what extent their visual quality was appreciated in those dark, gloomy and often smoke-filled interiors. The presence of those flowers was essentially functional – fashion for floral arrangements in the home only developed much later as domestic circumstances improved.

Rosa Gallica.　　　*Red Officinal Rose.*

flowers in the age of exploration

The 16th and 17th centuries were a time of immense cultural change. The discovery and exploration of the Americas and Asia resulted in extensive trading which not only brought about wealth but improved standards of living. The development of printing and easier communications aided the spread of knowledge and ideas, resulting in the cultural exchange of influences in art, architecture and garden design. The introduction of a wealth of new plants from America and the West Indies, South Africa and the Far East excited enormous interest. Being able to grow and display these novelties became a sign of social status and skills in propagation blossomed. The gardens of larger houses began to be fashionable places for outdoor recreation – and must have provided a welcome relief from the often gloomy and less than fragrant rooms inside.

■ FLORAL DISPLAYS FOR INTERIOR DECORATION

During the 17th and 18th centuries, houses became lighter and airier. Wealth accumulated through trade, and the home started to be used more for social gatherings and entertaining. As a result, interest in interior decoration became more intense. Domestic ornaments, including vases and containers, were not only more readily available but more affordable to a greater number of people. Decoration of the home with flowers and pot plants became more fashionable and visual effect became more important than the plants' aromatic qualities. (Improvements in domestic hygiene no

Helichrysum flowers from a 19th-century seed catalogue illustration.

doubt influenced this trend!) Pot-pourri, originally contained in fabric sachets for its scent, was attractively displayed in open bowls.

There was status to be gained in society houses by being able to display cut flowers and blooming pot plants throughout the winter and it was the head gardeners' task to ensure that these could be provided. By the beginning of the 19th century 'everlasting' flowers newly imported into Europe and America from Australia – strawflower

(*Helichrysum*), *Acroclineum* and *Rhodanthe* – were being made available through nurserymen's catalogues and listed specifically for their drying qualities. Flowers harvested from the 'cutting gardens' of big houses were dried specifically for use as *bouquets d'hiver*, or winter bouquets. It would have been possible to mimic the style of Dutch and Flemish still-life flower paintings, which were popular at that time, in which flowers of different flowering seasons were combined together in a classical vase for dramatic effect. Dried flowers, as floral displays in their own right, began to have a part to play.

■ DRYING AND PRESERVING IN THE HOME

Throughout these times the larger houses continued to maintain a 'still-room', presided over by the lady of the house and her housekeeper, where the skills of drying, preserving and processing were as important as before, though with a greater variety of plant material available.

In more humble homes the traditional varieties of dried flowers and herbs could still be found hanging from the beams providing that distinctive aroma of dried meadow hay. In public places it was still the custom to carry posies (known as 'tussie mussies') of sweet-smelling flowers and herbs to mask the unsavoury smells of the street and to ward off germs. In towns, the increased number of apothecaries and doctors meant that medicines were more readily available so there was less reliance on home-made potions.

flowers in the industrial age

With increased industrialization in the 19th century came more cramped living conditions in the towns and cities. Gardens were smaller and interest was increasing in the newly bred varieties of garden plants – tulips, carnations, dahlias, hydrangeas, and so on – but dried flowers and herbs were still needed for their scent and for cooking. Lavender was as popular as ever and regularly sold in the city streets.

The popularity of flowers for interior decoration throughout the house was increasing so much that there was also demand for artificial flowers made from fabric, wax or paper and for small displays on windowsills or mantelpieces.

■ EVERLASTING DISPLAYS

During the Victorian era – a time of feverish interest in imported plants, and equally feverish construction of greenhouses to accommodate them – interiors became rich and opulent, and could be almost oppressively cluttered with furniture and ornaments. There was a fascination for collecting and preserving objects like stuffed birds and animal trophies. Alongside these were displays of silk, wax and carved flowers, sometimes combined with 'everlastings' and protected under glass domes. The romantic symbolism associated with plants was taken very seriously and the Victorian 'Language of Flowers' was concerned not only with the individual species but with their colours and how the flowers were worn or arranged.

In this environment, dried flowers, including seed-heads and grasses, finally started to appear regularly as floral displays in their own right. The colour of the plant material used was probably not very bright but would have undoubtedly included such varieties as hydrangeas, honesty, *Allium* heads and *Helichrysum*. By the 19th century the readily available 'everlasting' flower varieties included *Amaranthus, Ammobium, Gomphrena,* and *Xeranthemum* together with ornamental grasses such as Pampas and Hare's tail. Other species popular as fresh garden flowers would also have been appreciated for their ability to retain colour when dried, especially the deep blue *Delphinium* and the glorious dark red *Paeonia officinalis*.

A London lavender seller from an engraving published in 1804.

flowers in the 20th century

The beginning of the 20th century heralded the development of a thriving cut-flower industry. Fewer large houses could afford the luxury of producing all their own flowers and vegetables. Most commodities including medicines were readily available, still-rooms became redundant and flower shops became a regular feature of the High Street. The drying of plants was no longer a domestic necessity, but was undertaken more for culinary use or for pleasure.

■ INFORMALITY AND CONVENIENCE

Interiors became simpler and less cluttered, and the influence of Japan and the Far East encouraged a more refined style of flower arranging. Single variety displays – even just of twigs in a simple container – became fashionable. There was also a general trend towards informality and natural items like teasels, poppy seed-heads and grasses were appreciated for their rustic charm.

Dried flowers became accessible to anyone and everyone and were especially suited to modern centrally heated homes. Bunches of home-grown honesty seed-pods and Chinese lanterns were supplemented by the colourful *Helichrysum* and *Limonium sinuatum*. Dried flowers were convenient. They usefully filled the autumnal gap between the last of the summer flowers and the Christmas decorations and were of course ideally suited to the celebration of harvest festivals and Thanksgiving. In the New Year they provided floral interest at a time when bought, imported cut flowers were expensive, and the daffodils were not yet out in the garden.

commercially dried flowers

THE NEED FOR CHANGE

However, the image of dried flowers up until the 1970s and 1980s was very much that of being a poor substitute for fresh flowers. Most flowers were merely hung upside down to dry, with little attention to picking stages or drying temperatures. The result was that the flowers had already lost some of their colour or were slightly past their best before they were even arranged. (The tendency was, and unfortunately too often still is, to then leave the display to fade still further and only to replace it when all colour had gone and the dust was too noticeable.) Most dried flowers were home-grown and the commercial production was only on a small scale with a limited number of varieties – essentially, the traditional 'everlastings'. This image changed radically with the advent of a commercial dried flower industry offering a wide range of varieties dried in specially designed kilns.

THE DUTCH INFLUENCE

During the 20th century the Dutch cut-flower industry expanded enormously (helped by low fuel costs and a tax system that favoured horticulture), and Holland became a central distribution point for cut flowers being imported into Europe from around the world. The inevitable variations in supply and demand meant that, at times, there was a surplus of certain flowers. It was realized that these could be purchased at very favourable rates and that their value could be increased by drying them and storing them for sale at a later date. Such

a system was particularly advantageous when handling high-value flowers such as roses. However, not all cut flowers could be treated in this way. The stage of bloom at which flowers are cut for the fresh flower trade is generally much earlier than is appropriate for flowers that have been grown to be dried.

The field-scale production of flowers specifically for drying was therefore developed and specialist knowledge built up on harvesting and drying techniques. With the large volume of plant material being processed it was necessary to use heat to speed up the drying process. This not only allowed a faster throughput of flowers, but held the colour better and maintained a higher quality appearance. Varieties were carefully selected that had the required characteristics of shape, texture, form and colour to appeal to florists and, to market the products, designers were employed to catch the imagination with new floral styles.

WORLD-WIDE ADVANCES

The growth in the production and marketing of dried flowers and preserved foliage in Holland was rapidly followed by the development of similar industries in the UK, Australia and America, with each country having its own range of favoured flowers. The availability of a wide range of dried flowers, of a quality not previously seen, created great excitement in the world of floristry and the rapid increase in demand led to yet more varieties being sourced and to adventurous new designs being created. Exotic seed-pods, stems and leaves

from the Far East, India, South America and South Africa began to be collected and distributed around the world.

INNOVATION IN DESIGN

Equally dramatic was the demand for new containers, and baskets of all shapes and sizes began to be imported from the Far East. There were new designs for metal or wire vases, terracotta pots and painted boxes – and as none of them had to be watertight, the possibilities were endless. Special dry foam bricks were developed to hold the flowers in place and the hot glue gun became an essential part of the flower arranger's equipment for securing in place the extra trimmings – shells, moss, dried fruit, spices and ribbons.

Spectacular and long-lasting designs – totally different to fresh arrangements – could be created simply by taking advantage of the fact that the dried flowers were not going to wilt and did not need to have their stems in water. The scope for unusual and original arrangements presented by dried flowers thus set new trends in fashion, and especially in interior decoration.

A truly modern and inter-national design. Chinese lantern heads glued to stems of English wheat, dyed and preserved oak leaves from France, and reindeer moss from Scandinavia. The pot is from the Far East.

DRIED FLOWERS FOR MODERN LIVING

Designers quickly discovered that flowers were versatile enough to enhance any setting from a rustic pine kitchen in a country cottage to an elegant Georgian living room. The range of flower types and colours could match any colour scheme (especially with the use of newly developed dyeing, painting and gilding techniques) and displays could therefore be used as finishing touches or focal points to a room. Frequent features in the media – magazines, craft journals and on the television – helped to increase the popularity and acceptance of dried flowers as an integral part of modern interior design. Not only were dried flowers ideal for centrally heated homes, but their longevity and cost-effectiveness also proved particularly attractive to busy working people. For other people, arranging dried flowers became a rewarding hobby which, in some cases, developed into small, home-based businesses.

COMMERCIAL USES OF DRIED FLOWERS

The type of elaborate floral displays normally only seen at society weddings or grand public occasions – such as swags and garlands – could be re-created in dried flowers for long-term display. This represented good value for money in prestige hotel or office reception areas, especially when compared to the cost of regularly replacing or tending fresh flowers and pot plants. Large, themed wall plaques or mirror surrounds became popular; these could

incorporate non-floral items such as gardening equipment (tools, pots, seed packets, twine and trugs), culinary accessories (wooden spoons, old sieves and spices in muslin bags) or seaside bric-à-brac (shells, rope and driftwood).

The gift trade adopted dried flowers as decorative elements, adding them to the packaging of toiletries, using them to adorn mirrors and frames and creating three-dimensional pictures and wall-hangings. Because flowers are so versatile in colouring and character, they were also used as part of shop merchandise displays to help sell all manner of other products.

TOWARDS A GREATER UNDERSTANDING

Design styles and colour combinations were adapted to suit national taste. For instance, bright bold colours were popular in the strong light of southern Europe whereas northern countries preferred more muted, natural tones. At one time, the 'European style' favoured formal linear ranks of flowers whereas the traditional 'English country garden' look with mixed selections of larkspur, peonies, roses and grasses, gave a loose and informal effect of universal appeal. Oriental, minimalist and geometric styles could also be catered for, especially with varieties such as corkscrew willow, textural wheat and seed-heads.

DRIED FLOWER SUCCESS

In the 1990s, dried flowers received the ultimate international seal of approval and acceptance into mainstream floral design when The Hop Shop won five consecutive Gold Medals at the Royal Horticultural Society's Chelsea Flower Show in London. Finally, the time had arrived for dried flowers to be appreciated as an art form in their own right.

With the quality of flowers now being produced commercially, and the ever-expanding range of sundries and containers available, the fashion is set to continue well into the 21st century. The main competition for dried flowers in the market-place is no longer from fresh ones but from fabric or 'silk' flowers, the best of which are so well made as to be easily mistaken for the real thing. But, fortunately, for discerning flower-lovers there is no substitute for nature's own beauty and the following chapters examine how many types of plant material can be preserved in their prime and displayed to maximum effect.

(facing page) Part of a Gold-Medal-winning display at the RHS Chelsea Flower Show. The scene is of cottage garden with 'grass' of dried moss, a 'herbaceous border' and a 'vegetable garden'.

PRODUCING

DRIED

FLOWERS

FOR SALE

the dried flower trade

During the second half of the 20th century, the popularity of dried flowers meant that production needed to move from a small-scale cottage garden industry to large commercial growing and drying units. The demand was not only for quantity but increasingly for quality, variety and – most importantly – for consistency of supply. To grow and dry a few bunches of flowers from the garden takes only a little time and skill. To produce a range of varieties of consistent bunch size and quality and to be able to supply them throughout the year needs a sound under-standing of customer requirements, detailed horticultural expertise in production, weed and pest control, availability of labour for harvesting, a great deal of management time backed up by financial investment in land, buildings and equipment... and the flexi-bility to respond to changing fashions.

◼ HOW QUALITY IS AFFECTED

There is far more skill and expertise in producing quality dried flowers than meets the eye. From the selection of seeds through their sowing, harvesting, drying, packing and transportation, many factors can affect quality. Having an understanding of these factors is of value to any grower or flower arranger interested in drying flowers at home or to anyone, whether florist or home-owner, who purchases dried flowers and wants to obtain the best products.

Consumers these days are, rightly, very exacting in their demands for top quality, but most people buying a bunch of dried flowers have no idea as to where or how those flowers were grown. The flowers could have originated in any of the six continents – exotic seed-pods or fungi from South America, giant poppies from India, *Banksia* from Australia, roses from Kenya, Colombia or Israel, sea lavender from the Mediterranean, moss from Scandinavia, or traditional garden flowers from England. The trade is truly international and the scale of production can range from one-man small-holdings to companies employing many people.

◼ INTERNATIONAL PRACTICES

In South America and the Far East many items for drying are collected from the wild; these comprise mainly seed-pods and ornamental stems which, being woody and neutral in colour, have no special drying requirements. They are required primarily for their form and may even be partly dry, so harvesting is easy and timing of it is not crucial. Any extra drying or treatment that is required is merely to ensure that residual moisture is removed to prevent rotting or insect damage during storage or transport. Very little capital expenditure is therefore necessary in the countries of origin.

However, when it is fresh flowers or other green plants that are being handled and dried commer-cially, the whole process becomes much more complex and demanding. If consistent quality is to be achieved, purpose-built drying and storage facilities are essential. These are mainly based in

Glass-house grown Helichrysum *need to be transplanted in the spring into specially prepared weed-free beds.*

Europe and North America. In the UK, members of the British Dried Flowers Association may grow anything from one to thirty hectares of flowers, but generally control all the production themselves and may have as many as fifty different types of flowers, grasses or herbs on offer. In Holland the major wholesalers control the drying, dyeing and storage facilities, but contract out much of the growing work to local farmers (supplying them with seed and instructions on production, and keeping a close watch throughout the growing season), and supplement this with bulk purchase of other varieties from abroad. In Australia, where many species are native ones growing in the wild, their harvesting is only allowed under licence.

Chinese lanterns, roses, apricot Limonium sinuatum *and golden rod (*Solidago*).*

varieties grown for drying

THE INFLUENCE OF FASHION

A producer's first job is to assess what the customers will be wanting each year and in what quantities. Predicting which colours and styles are going to be fashionable is not easy, especially since annual seeds need to be ordered maybe eighteen months before the final bunches are sold and perennials may take several years to establish. Fortunately, trends in home decor change less rapidly than in clothing styles!

SELECTION OF SPECIES

In addition to selecting the species appropriate to the grower's soil conditions, local climate and resources (of irrigation, buildings, labour and expertise), exact varieties need to be chosen with care to ensure that they are appropriate for drying. For instance, there are numerous shades of pink larkspur available for garden planting but some are too pale to hold their colour well when dried and others have florets too sparsely spaced up the stem to be effective. Similarly, *Nigella damascena* has one particular strain with a seed-pod more brightly striped than the others. Only a select few varieties combine all the right characteristics for commercial production.

The density of petals is also important; this not only applies to small flowers like *Achillea ptarmica* and *Gypsophila* but also to big ones such as peonies. All will shrink during the drying process, so it is important to start off with double-flowering varieties as these will be infinitely more effective than the single or semi-double types when dried. (The single *Gypsophila* flower is so tiny as to be an insignificant grey blur when dried, and the semi-double *Achillea ptarmica*, although it dries well, does not have the bright whiteness of the fully double form.) Spending time carefully nurturing a plant, only to discover that it is not quite as good as it could be, is both frustrating and expensive.

ACQUIRING THE SEEDS

Commercial producers usually purchase their seeds or young transplants from specialist nurserymen. (Saving home-produced seed is a time-consuming exercise and, in the long run, not generally considered to be cost effective.) A commercial grower does not want to risk poor germination or contamination by weed seeds, nor does he want inconsistency of growth form, height or colour. Uniformity is all important.

Sunflowers for drying need to be short and single-stemmed.

nurturing the plants

SOWING AND TRANSPLANTING

Some hardy annuals can be autumn-sown and, by over-wintering, have a head start over spring-sown seed. By maturing earlier the following year, the new season's crop can be marketed sooner. For similar reasons, a grower may choose to establish some plants of an important species from seed (maybe sowing successively over several weeks) and to raise other plants under glass to be planted out as soon as weather and soil conditions are favourable. The transplants come into flower some weeks earlier than the direct-sown ones. This extends the picking season – taking the pressure off at a busy time of year – and also acts as an insurance against unfavourable weather conditions which could cause problems at harvest-time.

Inevitably, transplanting is a much more expensive option than direct sowing, so generally it is only used when there are risks of poor germination or when a species is too tender for the local climate and needs warmth to germinate.

Weed control is a major problem in outdoor horticultural work. Seed-beds need to be clean of perennial weed contamination before establishment, and control of annual weeds must be vigorously maintained. Once a crop is growing, chemical weed control can be risky. In many cases, insufficient scientific trials have been done on the type of chemicals used to guarantee that flower crops will not be adversely affected. Mechanical hoeing and time-consuming hand-weeding are often the only options, and these are a significant element in overall production costs.

IRRIGATION

Irrigation may be required in dry seasons to ensure good establishment and growth. The soil needs to be checked for adequate levels of potassium and phosphate, but generally fertilizer applications are low compared with other crops. Plants raised on a soil too rich in nutrients tend to put on too much vegetative growth, making them 'leggy' and susceptible to wind-damage in exposed field conditions. Species such as lavender, thyme and marjoram positively thrive on thin, dry, stony soils which are akin to their native homelands around the Mediterranean.

DISEASES AND PESTS

A close watch needs to be kept for disease and pests. Rust fungi, *Botrytis* rot, pollen beetle, aphid and red spider mite (and that's just a short list) can all be a problem, discolouring stems or leaves, inhibiting growth and causing leaf-curl or petal drop. Some anti-fungal spraying may need to be done as a precaution against infection; for instance, mildew on larkspur may not become evident until close to flowering time, but by then it is too late to control and the visual quality of the plant material will have been severely impaired. Minor infections or infestations tend to be killed off by heat during kiln-drying.

Artichokes picked in bud open out to dry in glorious full flower.

harvesting

Harvesting is a tense time of daily monitoring – the condition of the plants and the weather… and the harvesting season for a big grower can last as long as five months. The following chapter on home-grown dried flowers covers in detail the picking requirements for individual species but the general principles are covered here in relation to commercial cropping.

▨ WHEN TO HARVEST

Fresh flowers cut for the commercial market are invariably cropped in bud or early flower with the intention that they reach their prime several days later having been been packed, transported, maybe cold stored, sold on via a market or auction and progressed through a florist to a finished arrangement where they are finally expected to develop into full flower and look their best. With dried flowers, the picking stages have to be related much more closely to what is wanted for the final appearance, bearing in mind that their development is going to be halted by the drying process.

Because dried flowers are a preserved rather than a living, changing form, their value is in their specific attributes of colour, texture, shape or size. They need, therefore, to be picked at whatever is the best stage to maximize these qualities for their intended use. Their individual qualities may be the texture of the bud (*Echinops*), the colour of the petals (roses), the height of the flower stem (larkspur), the shape of the seed-pod (poppy), the overall size (artichokes) and so on. Most flowers fit into only one category, though wheat, for instance, can be picked green at the flowering stage or later when golden and filled with grain.

But it is not enough just to know in advance what the end product should look like – a grower must understand what changes to the plants' appearance will take place during the drying process. Plant material that is naturally woody, papery or fine-stemmed contains little moisture and so will dry quickly, changing little in the process. A plant that is dense, fleshy or in full vegetative growth contains more moisture or sap, so will take longer to dry and will continue to develop during the drying process. It needs, therefore, to be picked at an earlier stage to allow for those changes to take place. Through experience (which includes trial and error) and by knowing the effectiveness of their drying facilities, growers can fine-tune the harvesting stage of different species to suit the drying speeds of the kilns so that the result is the best possible quality.

This fine-tuning may need to be specific to an exact day of picking – a delay of only twenty-four hours can be critical to a fast-blooming peony or *Echinops* on the verge of breaking bud. Bearing in mind how crucial good weather is at harvest-time, the grower is involved in a continual juggling act between the needs of the crop, the vagaries of the forecast, availability of labour for picking and space for drying. A sudden thunderstorm or a mechanical breakdown at a critical time can spell the difference between a first- or second-grade crop… or no crop at all. Delays result in flowers developing beyond the required stage, losing colour or dropping petals.

Larkspur at the height of the cropping season needs picking selectively every few days .

Pre-harvest crops of millet, Amaranthus, Lonas *(African Daisy) and statice with larkspur in the background.*

METHODS OF HARVESTING

Given an untroubled growing season, most annual species are uniform in growth and maturity and, if cut in full flower or seed-pod stage, can often be taken in a block, for instance *Nigella, Carthamus,* linseed, grasses and poppies. Once the majority of the crop is at the right stage, the whole area will be cut. Annuals taken in early flower, such as larkspur or cornflower, need to be cut selectively. *Helichrysum* grows again from lateral shoots after the leader has been taken and can thus be cropped repeatedly over several months. Most perennials, like *Achillea filipendulina, Centaurea* and artichokes, have flowers at differing stages of development over a longer period of time. These need to be selectively cropped at least twice a week until all the good specimens have been taken.

SIZING THE BUNCHES

The cutting of the flowers requires detailed instructions being given to the pickers and close supervision of quality. Virtually all flowers and grasses are cut and bunched by hand in the field. With a wide range of flower types, each having precise specifications for bunch size, stem length and final appearance, it is very difficult to mechanize the work effectively – even with those varieties that are cut in a block. A machine is only used occasionally.

The bunch sizes are predetermined for each individual variety (usually conforming to accepted standards within the trade) and, once set, need to remain consistent. A bunch may be measured by the number of stems or flower-heads or by its bulk as a handful – the latter being the most difficult to achieve consistently especially when the members of a picking gang have widely differing hand sizes!

Account also needs to be taken of seasonal changes in growth. *Helichrysum* at the start of the season have thick, juicy stems that may bear several heads. Later cropping of the lateral shoots yields thinner, single-flowered stems of which more are needed to make up a bunch of equivalent size.

Apart from the cost of having to adjust wrongly sized bunches, trying to correct bunches after they have been dried can cause damage. The aim is to achieve the correct size from the start and to maintain that standard consistently, remembering that the size of a fresh bunch may be very different from the same one when dried. The volume of fleshy stems may be reduced by over a half.

The cutting of Echinops *in bud needs to be especially selective to ensure only the best specimens are dried.*

ARRANGING THE STEMS

A grower also has to work backwards from what the final product should look like to know how to arrange the stems. The stem length and the presentation of the final bunch are all-important to its saleability to a prospective customer. The flower-heads need to be grouped together for best impact, rather than being at different heights in the bunch. However, large heads such as *Achillea* or peonies need to be staggered slightly so that they overlap, otherwise they do not pack well into boxes for storage.

Because of the shrinkage, the fresh bunches need to be tightly bound with rubber bands. The bands must be strong enough not to perish quickly and to have enough elasticity to be wound two or three times around the stems so that they remain secure during drying.

THE EFFECTS OF WEATHER

Hot, sunny weather brings the flowers into bloom quickly and the job of picking can be a race against time to ensure that everything is cut in prime condition. Dull, cold weather slows down the flowering process and can be a particular problem when it causes uneven flowering. *Carthamus*, for instance, has branched stems supporting many buds; the leader stem comes into flower first and, in sunny weather is rapidly followed by the others, so it can be cut when a high percentage (maybe 90 percent) are in full flower. If the weather is cold and wet the first flower will start to die off and the others emerge slowly, so there may be some flowers going over, some in full bloom, some just emerging and some still in green bud. The resultant effect is disappointing but there is nothing that a grower can do about it.

Rain damages delicate petals and can drastically affect the colour, especially of *Statice sinuata*. It can cause fungal problems on stems, leaves and seed-heads, but its main disruption is to the harvesting process. Picking can only take place when the weather is dry. If wet bunches are put into the kilns the increase in humidity radically slows down the drying process, causing green stems and leaves to turn yellow and flower petals to discolour. It is far better to let the sun and the wind remove some of the moisture first.

A trailer-load of cardoons being bunched and hung.

the commercial drying process

In the past, when the quantity and range of flowers being handled was smaller and quality expectations were not so high, small-scale growers would hang bunches in the roof space of barns and outbuildings and allow ambient air conditions to do the drying. Now, the need for the fast throughput of large volumes of succulent material and the demands for good colour retention necessitate more sophisticated facilities. (In hot, dry countries or where woody material is being handled, ambient air temperatures may be sufficient to achieve the necessary speed of drying.)

DRYING IN KILNS

Most commercial growers have purpose-built systems based on the bunches being hung upside down in temperature-controlled kilns. The fresh bunches are spiked on to metal rods which are then supported on specially designed trolleys ready to be wheeled into the room-sized kilns. It is essential for best colour retention that the drying process is started as soon as possible, so all the flowers picked during the day must be safely in the kilns by evening. Big ceiling fans are used to circulate the hot air and ensure even drying and extractor fans remove wet air. Some drying systems rely on dehumidification rather than heat but this is generally not fast enough as a method on its own to retain top quality colour.

Linseed drying in the kiln.

Freshly cut flowers, already spiked onto metal rods, are loaded on to trolleys ready to be wheeled into the kilns for drying.

TIMING AND TEMPERATURE

Flowers must be dried quickly, firstly to hold good colour throughout the bunch, and secondly to allow a fast throughput so that the kilns can receive the next batch; harvesting in the field cannot afford to wait for kiln space to become available. Temperatures are set as high as possible, but a balance needs to be achieved between fast drying and loss of quality. Wheat, for instance, will lose its fresh greenness and turn yellow if not dried quickly but, on the other hand, will look dull and flat if the temperature has been too high. *Helichrysum*, which has fat juicy stems, needs to dry fast enough to prevent the flowers over-maturing. However, *Achillea ptarmica* and white-flowered varieties of peony and larkspur can discolour to a creamy or parchment shade if the temperature and humidity are too high. The aim is to dry the flowers not cook them.

Very dense items, like artichokes, benefit most from gentle drying, which allows them to develop into full flower gradually during the drying process. Their solidity is such that the moisture can only be drawn out of them relatively slowly. The same is true of Chinese lanterns – the papery orange seed-pods hardly need drying at all, but the central fruit takes a surprisingly long time to shrivel to a stage where it can be safely packed for storage. Chinese lanterns fortunately are one of the latest crops to be harvested in the autumn so there is less urgency to move them on from the kilns.

'Dumosa' reacts adversely to heat – the flowering stems arch and become brittle. Like other varieties of *limonium*, it contains very little moisture, so does not change much during drying. By slow drying it without heat, its natural springiness can be retained, making it much more attractive and easier to use.

alternative methods of drying

TESTING DRYNESS

Drying times can vary from a few days for poppies to several weeks for artichokes, but it is essential that everything is fully dry before being packed away for storage. Knowing how to test for dryness is, in itself, an art, and unless correctly mastered has unfortunate consequences in the form of rapid development of mould. It is always the densest part of a bunch or flower-head which is tested; with many species this is the centre of the bunch under the rubber band. If dry, individual stems will snap easily rather than bend. The critical point on sunflowers or artichokes is the base of the head where it joins the stem – carefully attempting to insert a sharp knife will reveal any areas of softness. With *Carthamus* it is the insides of the flowering heads that need to be examined and 'rubbed out'. If they are dry, the newly forming seeds will readily detach themselves from the base of the flower-head, which itself will snap if bent. Seeds can sometimes be a site where moulds develop in storage and the oily seeds of linseed, in particular, can be very deceptive, needing slow drying long after the stems are bone dry.

With a trolley-load of flowers, care must be taken to test bunches hanging in the centre and on lower rails since they will have experienced slightly lower temperatures and less air circulation than other bunches and there may have been different rates of drying.

PRESERVING AND GLYCERINING

The principle of glycerining is to replace the water in the plant's tissues with a mixture of glycerine and water. The method inevitably dulls any natural colour, but it is most useful for preserving foliage that would otherwise shrivel or be too brittle if conventionally dried. The fresh-cut mature foliage is stood in the liquid until the natural process of transpiration has drawn up the glycerine through to the leaves. Colour can be added to the glycerine to enhance greens or to give variations on browns and burgundies. Preserved foliage is valuable as background filler material for large displays or, alternatively, the individual leaves can be removed and used decoratively (see the oak leaves around the pot of Chinese lanterns on page 21). Beech, oak, and eucalyptus are the most popular commercial species.

New methods of preservation are continually being researched to achieve fresh-looking flowers that have a long life. Most of these processes are expensive and therefore only worthwhile on high value items.

FREEZE-DRYING

Freeze-dryers are expensive items of equipment but produce glorious results on a range of plants from flowers to fruit and fungi. Normal freezing tends to break down cell walls so that, once defrosted, the structure is not maintained. By taking the moisture out of the plants simulta-neously the cell wall structure is retained in its original shape. Space inside a freeze-drier is at a premium, with the flowers being laid on trays. It is only economically viable therefore to dry individual heads rather than bunches, but roses, rose petals, peonies, lilies and *Narcissi* all work successfully. The only problem is that the resultant flowers are so perfect that handling, packaging and trans-porting them without damage needs great care.

SILICA-DRYING

Though achieving glorious results on flowers with delicate petals like peonies, silica drying takes a lot of space and time and is not generally considered to be commercially viable. It is, however, a very appropriate and successful method for drying a range of garden varieties at home and is described more fully in the next chapter.

A full-headed garden rose is a good candidate for silica-drying.

further treatments

DYEING

The dyeing of flowers obviously increases their versatility for co-ordinating with interior colour schemes and the process can be adapted to suit current fashions. Dyeing is carried out on plant material that is already dried and most growers do this during the winter months when time, labour and kiln-space are available after the urgency of harvest is past. The bunches are first dipped into a fixer and then into the dye. The surface of some plant material such as *Carthamus* or wheat may resist the dye and heat may be needed to assist the process. The dyed bunches are then hung up to dry again, which takes only a short time.

Individual varieties can react differently to the same dye colour so experimentation is necessary. It is possible to achieve delicate pastel shades of peach, pink and lavender blue on white or pale-coloured petals, such as *Gypsophila, Limonium dumosum* and *Achillea ptarmica*, and, if subtly used, the colours can look quite natural. Green plant material – stems, leaves and buds – will tone down the colour of any dye it absorbs, but the use of shades such as terracotta or burgundy can produce excellent background colours which remain strong over a much longer time than the original green. Dyed *Carthamus* and wheat are especially useful, being sturdy and good fillers. Interesting effects can also be achieved by using dyes on coloured flowers; for instance, red dye on yellow *Achillea filipendulina* produces a wonderful burnt orange colour. Take care also when using dyed flowers as some strong colours can stain hands or fabrics.

Poppies surface-coated with white paint can add variations of colour as well as form.

Note that dye effects vary with each variety. Bright or exact colours can only be achieved by first bleaching the plant material to remove its natural colour. The effected produced will always look artificial. For this and for environmental reasons this process is avoided by most growers.

SURFACE-COATING AND SPRAY-PAINTING

Dipping bunches into paint mixtures can also successfully produce unusual shades, such as opaque pastel colours and frosted, gold or glitter effects. Elegant burnished or 'antique' effects can be achieved by double-dipping – first into a colour and then into dull gold.

On a small scale, cans of spray paint or glitter are easy to use on the flowers or indeed the containers so the latter are fully co-ordinated into the display. In the picture above the eucalyptus leaves have been given a light dusting of white spray paint to give them a wintery effect. Poppies do not easily take up dye but are good candidates for coating or spraying with paint. Their strong form makes them particularly dramatic.

packing for storage

The obvious problem with handling, packing and transporting flowers that are bone dry is the damage that results from their brittleness – petals and stems being broken, leaves disintegrating and heads being knocked off. A solution is to let the trolleys stand out of the kilns to 'condition' for a short while. By naturally absorbing a small amount of atmospheric moisture, the bunches soften and become less fragile to handle. But in weather conditions of high humidity they can easily take in too much water and need to be returned to the kiln for a short period!

▨ QUALITY CONTROL

Quality control – ensuring that bunch size, colour and dryness are all correct – is crucial at this stage. Methods of packing vary for individual species to ensure that delicate heads are not crushed while fitting the maximum number of bunches into a box. Once sealed with tape, the cardboard boxes can then be labelled for identification and to provide batch referencing to record any seasonal variations in quality.

storage

Safe storage is essential in commercial units, especially since sales take place over a period of twelve months. Buildings are better if insulated and the use of dehumidifiers is often required. Dampness rapidly encourages mould and even slight rises in atmospheric moisture can cause problems, making petals limp and discolouring leaves and stems.

▨ PROTECTION FROM PESTS

During any period of storage, the flowers are vulnerable to damage from pests. Mice are the most frequent culprits – a dried flower store is not only a wonderful larder of seeds (poppy, linseed, wheat, oats, millet) but also a delightful source of colour co-ordinated bedding material!

The presence of warehouse moths can be even more damaging. First the extent of damage is more difficult to detect until it is too late, second the problem is more difficult to eradicate and third the moth has a costly taste for high value roses and peonies! This insect, which resembles an ordinary clothes moth, loves the dry conditions of a store. In the late spring it lays its eggs in the flower-heads, which provide a source of food for the young larvae when they hatch out later in the year. (Hatching may be instigated by slight rises in humidity during the autumn or winter.) The eggs are almost impossible to detect, but the droppings or 'frass', which can be mistaken for tiny eggs, are often coloured by the petals. The larvae eat away the

Careful packing ensures bunches retain quality in transit.

base of the petals causing the flower-heads to disintegrate. The larvae may then migrate to other parts of the store to pupate and wait to hatch out the following year when the air is warmer. Eradication of moths in the breeding season, backed up by the use of moth deterrent chemicals (such as mothballs) in the boxes of susceptible species, needs to be accompanied by good store hygiene.

transportation

Settlement can occur during storage, so repacking is sometimes necessary before transportation to ensure that the contents withstand being handled by modern conveyor-belt sorting systems. Bunches may be damaged if there is space for them to move around – heads can be crushed and fragile flowers broken by friction.

A box of flowers may not weigh much but it is proportionately very bulky. Transport costs, expecially for air freight, are based on volume and costs can therefore be discouragingly high.

▨ EXPORTING DRIED FLOWERS

Dried flowers are subject to strict customs regulations in certain countries even though the risk of disease transference is far lower than for growing plants and fresh-cut flowers. Treatment with pesticides is sometimes required before export. Many countries restrict import of cereal

selling dried flowers

Dried flowers are now seen for sale not just in florists' shops and at craft fairs but in department stores, markets, garden centres, supermarkets, gift shops and even the forecourts of petrol stations. Needless to say, the quality can be questionable in some of these outlets and the conditions in which the flowers are displayed and handled may not always be conducive to keeping the quality that a grower has worked so hard to achieve. It is important for retailers to understand what can be detrimental to the flowers and for customers to be discerning in the quality that they buy.

■ PRACTICAL CONSIDERATIONS

The three factors that shorten shelf-life are: high humidity, exposure to sunlight and rough handling. Inevitably, flowers on display in the open are likely to absorb any humidity in the air. This can be mitigated by the use of cellophane sleeves or wrappers but flowers that get damp can droop and will also tend to lose colour more quickly. Unfortunately humidity is also high inside shops selling fresh flowers and the two do not mix together happily. Separate areas – both for display and storage – ought to be designated for the dried flowers. Small florists' shops need to aim for a limited stock with a fast turnover or to select seed-heads, grasses and varieties such as golden yarrow which are least affected by humidity.

Dried flowers should not be displayed in direct sunlight as fading, due to the effect of ultraviolet on chlorophyll, is rapid. Shop windows or glass roofed garden centres are both inappropriate

crops, such as wheat, barley, oats and maize, because of the risk of spreading diseases damaging to the local agricultural economy. Inevitably, most customs authorities are highly sensitive to the

presence in a consignment of *Papaver somniferum*, the opium poppy, even though the dried plant material, when grown in temperate climates, has only a decorative use in arrangements.

unless shade is provided or the displays are changed frequently. Exotic varieties that are neutral or brown in colour or plant material reliant on shape for visual impact (poppies, artichokes, maize cobs) are more appropriate in these very bright locations than dried 'garden' flowers. Grasses, except those harvested at the golden stage, should never be displayed in bright sunlight. *Helichrysum* and statice have such strong colour that they can withstand sunlight for a long time without too deleterious an effect, but the fading of the stem colour is nevertheless apparent in time.

Attractive though it may be to display the flowers as naturally as possible, it is always advisable to sleeve dried flowers in paper or cellophane for retail display. This not only protects them from damage when being handled by customers but also keeps off the dust and makes pricing easier. Additionally, it gives protection from prickles or thorns – teasels, carline thistles, roses and *Echinops* are not known for being customer-friendly. Faded or battered flowers should always be removed and displays frequently refreshed.

Delicate varieties such as *Echinops* and roses should be located where they will not be damaged by people passing by, and any sharp or spiny items put out of reach of small children.

■ EFFECTIVE DISPLAY

Many retailers display dried flowers in baskets because the size and shape of the containers can be selected to suit the stem length of each species. A popular system for display has also been 'pigeon holes' which allow the flowers to be grouped by colour. This can look marvellous if the display is regularly tended. The problem is that delicate flowers can be damaged by the weight of other bunches on top of them, and the whole effect can be rapidly disrupted by bunches being continually taken out and replaced – not always in the correct place. Whatever system is used, one of the most important rules is to display dried flowers as a mass of colour. Better sales are achieved by having a limited number of species, selected for colour and texture and carefully grouped together, than by mixing assorted flowers.

Since dried flowers need to be displayed boldly to achieve visual impact it is important to make sure that bunch sizes are generous. For each species, there is a specific size that just feels and looks right, and the way they are presented should enhance this.

■ PURCHASERS' REQUIREMENTS

Ideally, knowledgeable staff should always be on hand to give advice. The successful retailing of dried flowers requires specialist knowledge, not only of the individual species and their aftercare, but of how to select bunches to make up a finished arrangement. Many people purchasing fresh flowers will buy on impulse because of a particular flower's colour or seasonal appeal and they will often buy only a single variety or a ready-made mixed bouquet. Because fresh flowers are short lived, co-ordinating them to interior decor is not so crucial. However, when purchasing dried flowers, a customer is thinking about how the flowers will fit into the home in the longer term. Far more attention is paid to colour and, often, it is not just a single flower type but a combination of bunches which is wanted to create a particular effect.

Selecting the right species takes skill and experience. An understanding is needed of how the colours, shapes and textures work together and the quantities of material needed to make a display of a particular size or character. A self-service system of retailing rarely results in a satisfied customer.

■ HOW A FLORIST CAN HELP

Inventive florists should be able to give inspiration on seasonal themes, colour combinations, designs, the use of new products and the addition of trimmings such as ribbons or bows, as well as advising on the technical construction of a display. Unfortunately the training most floristry students have received in the past has been heavily weighted towards fresh flowers, and their familiarity and expertise with dried materials is often very limited. Dried flowers cannot be handled in the same way as fresh ones, and a radically different approach to arranging is needed to achieve the best and most original results. (Many successful arrangers of dried flowers come from an art or craft background rather than floristry.) Staff training is therefore crucial to ensure familiarity with the range of dried plant material available, how it is produced, how to recognize quality, how to display it to best advantage and how to advise on aftercare in the home.

identifying quality

Without quality materials to begin with, no display can look its best. Broken stems and damaged heads are obvious signs of poor handling, but there are other signs too. Strength of colour can be deceptive – gradual fading may only become apparent when comparing a freshly dried bunch with old stock. It is always worth checking colour in daylight.

■ HOW 'DRY' ARE THE FLOWERS?

Over-dry flowers may feel brittle to the touch and be fragile. The problem can usually be solved by using a fine mist spray to soften them before handling. Dried hop bines benefit from being left overnight in a damp atmosphere (not outside, but in a shed or garage) where they can absorb some moisture which makes them much easier to handle. The centre stem may still remain brittle but the flowers will behave less like confetti.

Flowers stored in damp conditions may feel soft or dank to the touch. *Helichrysum* which have absorbed a little too much moisture during storage or on retail display will tend to droop because the heads are large and the stems have no woody structure to support their weight. Hanging the bunches upside down in a dry atmosphere for a short while will quickly remedy the problem.

Having read this book, no one should be in any doubt as to the standards that can be achieved and should be demanded wherever and whenever dried flowers are purchased.

Dried sunflowers as an art form.

GROWING AND DRYING AT HOME

air-drying at home

Drying flowers at home is a thoroughly worthwhile and enjoyable pastime for anyone who loves their garden. It preserves nature's bounty and transfers it into the house to give pleasure throughout the year – whether it is fresh bunches hanging to dry in the kitchen or finished arrangements in the living room.

But part of the pleasure comes from the increased understanding and awareness of the flowers themselves. Producing good quality dried flowers means preserving them in their prime and this challenge is great fun. To preserve flowers that are of aesthetic value for arranging, it is essential to understand what is being aimed for in the final product so that the best characteristics can be retained by whatever method of drying is appropriate. The skill is to make the most of the plants and the drying facilities that are available – selecting the best varieties, cutting them at the right time, drying them to retain their best characteristics and then displaying them to advantage.

In the following pages I explore the general guidelines for air-drying and storing flowers at home and describe other methods of preservation.

An airing cupboard is an ideal place to dry flowers at home. Most need to be hung upside down. (top row, left to right) Achillea filipendulina, Acroclineum, Delphinium consolida, Lonas; (*bottom row*) Lavender, Nigella damascena, Cynara scolymus.

The greater part of the chapter is devoted to a review of the most popular, common or successful plants used for drying. They have been grouped according to the stage at which they should be harvested since this is the key to success. The intention is that the underlying principles can then be applied to other plants.

Serious drying of flowers takes space, and the harvesting period can last many months, so plan ahead to make sure you have the right facilities to dry all you want. A dry, dark location with a good circulation of warm or hot air is essential. A large airing cupboard is useful because the slatted shelves allow the air to move freely. Attics are also successful for drying during the summer but may not be suitable – either because of damp or mice – for storage later in the year. Because of the likelihood of moths in an attic, the use of insect repellents or mothballs (which also deter mice) is advisable.

Small quantities of flowers can be hung over boilers or radiators and many people like to use the old-fashioned clothes racks suspended from the ceiling. Flowers dried like this in a kitchen may not retain as good a colour as those dried in the dark, but their decorative effect can be enjoyed during the drying process. Drying at the back of large cookers is quick and effective but the bunches tend to pick up greasy dust.

Greenhouses or conservatories should not be used for drying because of the bright light; garages, outhouses or cellars are too damp. Bunches can quickly go mouldy and, moreover, slow drying in a damp atmosphere results in significant colour loss.

Flowers should be picked when the weather is dry, preferably during sunshine and not while still wet after rain. They should be taken inside, away from direct light, as soon as possible. Unwanted leaves can be stripped, but do not remove them all – they are useful fillers. Keep the bunches small to allow them to dry quickly, and secure them with string, raffia or rubber bands. Tie them near the base of the stems so that the heads are not crushed together and the stems hang vertically. Most species need to be hung upside down to prevent the heads drooping, but some woody stemmed varieties, such as cardoons or artichokes, can be supported upright. Common sense is needed with a species that has a trailing or hanging form; for instance, Chinese lanterns are best dried upright to prevent the heads breaking off.

Testing the absolute dryness of the flowers is not especially crucial in the home – it is far more important commercially when flowers are being packed for storage. Nevertheless the specific tips given in this chapter are useful guidelines. The flowers can be deceptive – appearing dry when they are not – and may deteriorate in quality if stored before they are ready or tend to droop if used upright in an arrangement.

On a personal note, if I am uncertain as to dryness, I try testing the plant material gently against my lower lip which quickly detects both moisture and temperature. But don't try this with prickly or spiky plants or anything likely to cause an adverse or allergic reaction.

drying with silica and glycerine

SILICA-DRYING

Because silica-drying is time-consuming and takes a lot of space it is not generally considered to be commercially viable, except perhaps with peonies, but it is a particularly appropriate method for drying at home, achieving reliable and stunning results with the minimum of outlay.

The method is most appropriate for those flowers that have delicate petals or distinct forms which would not hold their shape with air-drying. Many of the spring flowers, such as freesias, tulips and daffodils, fall into this category and even the small heads of *Narcissi* can make a delightful ingredient in pot-pourri mixes. Flowers like lilies and *Clematis* which cannot be air-dried because they shrivel retain their characteristic shape much better when dried in silica.

Silica-drying is particularly satisfying when used for large showy heads of peonies or old-fashioned garden roses. These can be huge, and even though they can be air-dried their bulk is greatly reduced as the petals shrivel. Silica crystals help to maintain their size and shape so the blooms can then be used as focal flowers for prestigious displays. Silica crystals are readily available and some are treated to change colour, indicating if they are fully dry or contain moisture.

The plant material should be free of rain or dew when cut and the picking stage should correspond with the principles of picking for air-drying – that is, sometimes allowing for development to take place during the drying process. The drying of large peony blooms is described on page 104.

Plastic boxes are ideal containers for silica-drying. A layer of crystals should be spread over the base. The stalks should be trimmed and any wiring necessary for later design work done while the flowers are fresh as they will be too fragile later. The heads should be laid down gently and crystals spooned carefully between the petals to retain their form. When completely covered in crystals the box can be put in a warm, dry, dark place.

Drying can take anything from a few days to a couple of weeks, depending on the size and moisture content of the plant material. It is like discovering buried treasure when the time comes to uncover the flowers and see how perfectly they have been preserved. When completely dry, the petals are very fragile and the blooms need to be removed and displayed with the utmost care. A low level of atmospheric moisture will soften the petals but damp air will make them droop.

The crystals can be reused after drying out, but be careful how and where you store them – some silica looks just like sugar.

PRESERVING WITH GLYCERINE

Glycerine is useful for retaining the suppleness of both deciduous and evergreen foliage, such as ivy, laurel, magnolia, eucalyptus, oak, beech, and many more. The foliage should be cut while the sap is still rising and the stems battered to help absorption. Mix the glycerine with hot water in a sturdy container and stir well. A ratio of 1:2 of glycerine to water is usual though sometimes equal quantities are used. Leave the plant material to

stand in a dark place for one to two weeks until the glycerine has been drawn up into the leaves. The process usually darkens the natural leaf colour.

Dye can be added to the glycerine. Commercially, burgundy, emerald green and rich brown dyes are frequently used, but at home it may be better just to think in terms of enhancing the foliage's natural colour with a dye rather than trying to change its appearance radically.

storage – general rules

Ideally the flowers should be displayed when they are at their best – freshly-dried – and the autumn and winter were traditionally the times when dried flowers were most in demand for the home. However, the fashion for having colour co-ordinated floral displays as a permanent part of interior design schemes has meant that commercially it is necessary to store them for up to a year so that they are available whenever required.

Most of the flowers described in this book can be stored for long periods without significant loss of quality, although the vibrancy of some colours diminishes over time. Light pink peonies will

Tulips, lilies and Narcissus *'Soleil d'Or' are good candidates for drying in silica and are shown here with commercially grown roses.*

gradually pale and greens become less rich though the difference may not be noticeable unless direct comparisons are made with freshly dried material. *Helichrysum* heads can remain unchanged for several years and it may be only the colour of the stems which indicates their age. Similarly, dark blue larkspur holds its rich shades surprisingly well. Neutral-coloured items like poppies or golden oats do not alter.

If space, dust and light are not a problem, the bunches can be left to hang where they dried. If they need to be stored they should be laid gently in cardboard boxes with the heaviest items at the bottom to prevent crushing. Delicate flowers can be kept separate by layers of tissue paper. Boxes should be well sealed and labelled with the contents. Carry and store boxes horizontally.

Storage should always be in dark, dry locations. Garages or garden sheds should not be used as damp will soon penetrate and cause mould. Insulated attics are ideal but not if mice are present: flowers with seeds, such as poppies, linseed and wheat, are an obvious source of food and other plants, like the hare's tail grass, provide desirable bedding material. Certain plants containing camphor reputedly act as deterrents to mice and it is advisable to put mothballs in the boxes to discourage not only mice but also moths who may lay their eggs in the flowers. Moth larvae can cause devastation among dried flowers; once an area is infested it is very difficult to eradicate the problem. Hanging insect repellents in the storage area during the spring and summer will also help to deter the adult moths.

suitability of plant material for drying

Most grasses are easier to dry at home if cut at the golden stage rather than at the green.

An appreciation of the physical qualities of the plant material being handled, and the way that it can change during the drying process, is valuable to the home enthusiast as well as being essential information for serious students of floristry and commercial growers. So, before starting, be aware of each plant's structure and character so that its attributes of colour and textural form can be enhanced and its shortcomings minimized.

▪ COLOUR

The drying process changes all colours. A plant's ability to retain good colour both during the drying process and afterwards in display is very important. Do not forget that the stem, leaves and buds can be just as important to the overall effect as the petals.

1 Select varieties that have the best and strongest colour. For instance, some pink varieties of larkspur are more vibrant than others and some *Nigella* seed-pods have more interesting stripes.

2 If possible, select double rather than single-flowered varieties to compensate for shrinkage.

3 Be aware of how weather conditions at harvest, the speed of drying and subsequent exposure to light can affect colour retention.

▪ STRUCTURE

Since all living plants contain water and since the drying process is designed to remove that water, it is obviously essential that the plant's structure can cope with this radical change.

1 Woody or densely structured forms will obviously hold their shape very well when the moisture is removed. Some, such as the hollow stems of teasel or the petals of *Helichrysum*, may contain very little moisture even when fresh. Other species, such as poppies or hydrangeas, picked at the end of their growing season, have already started to dry out naturally.

2 Fleshy plant material changes rather more radically when dried – petals shrink, leaves curl and stems lose their strength. Timing when the plant is cut can be critical to ensure that, for instance, the petals of peonies have reached their optimum size, that leaves of eucalyptus are mature, or that stem tips of lavender or *Amaranthus* have developed enough structure to stay upright and not droop.

3 If petals shrivel to the extent that the form of a flower is lost, it may be necessary to consider drying with silica rather than air.

4 When stems contain a lot of sap the drying will take longer, resulting in colour loss (especially a dulling from bright to pale or yellow-green). An increase in drying temperatures or air movement may be necessary to compensate for this. Another important effect is that the flowers will continue to develop during the drying process. This may not be a problem with a versatile flower like an artichoke but is a real problem with the quality of *Helichrysum*. This change needs to be allowed for by picking the plant at an earlier stage.

5 Fleshy stems have a weak structure when dried and therefore need careful handling; they may need wiring or other support in a display.

6 The way petals or leaves are attached to a plant affects its suitability for air-drying or may determine the time of picking. Peonies in full bloom will rapidly drop their petals so need early picking and fast drying. Certain eucalyptus varieties are best preserved with glycerine to retain their suppleness and prevent leaf-drop.

▪ A FEW WORDS OF WARNING

Thorns or bristles which are sharp on a fresh plant can be even more vicious when the item is dried. If possible, it is a good idea to remove problem leaves before drying and to use gloves if necessary when arranging with the bunches afterwards.

Pollen may cause hay-fever when flowers are being harvested and sometimes mild skin irritation during subsequent handling.

deciding when to harvest

Before you start, it is important to know exactly what you want to achieve and why. Also remember that the attributes for which a dried flower is valued may be very different to the qualities that give it charm as a fresh flower.

Each piece of plant material that is used for a decorative purpose will have a particular feature for which it is chosen. This may be its shape, size, texture, aroma or colour. The aim of drying or preserving any part of a plant is to retain or enhance these specific characteristics. With a flowering plant this may be when it is in bud, in early flower or full bloom, or when it has developed a seed-head. With a tree species it may be when it is in full leaf or when the branches are bare.

It is also helpful to have some understanding of the simple botanical structure of a plant, so that the subtle changes that take place during its growth can be predicted, thus enabling the time of harvesting to be fine-tuned to an exact stage of the plant's development. For instance, a poppy cannot be cropped as soon as it forms a seed-head because its structure is too soft. It will shrivel when dried and not retain such an attractive full spherical shape. It is necessary to wait until it develops a degree of maturity evidenced by subtle colour changes.

The decision of when to pick is also influenced by the type of drying facilities available. If temperatures are low and air movement restricted, the drying process takes longer. Bunches should therefore be smaller and allowances made for the earlier cropping of flowers that have a critical picking time, like *Echinops* and peonies, or that are fleshy and continue to change, like *Helichrysum*. Different locations in the home will suit different varieties – the best knowledge comes from experimentation.

Several weeks of bright sunshine have brought this statice into full flower.

species to be harvested in bud

Some species are cut in bud to preserve particular qualities of shape or colour. Invariably plants that are cut in bud need to have developed to a stage just before they burst into flower:

1 To ensure that the bud is as large and mature as it will get so that it does not shrivel when dried.

2 To give time for the bud to develop as much colour as possible, most important with *Echinops*.

3 To make sure the stem has hardened enough to support the flower. On some plants, while the stem is still growing and the buds are developing, the top of the stem is fleshy and soft. Just before the flowers open, the stem becomes woodier – presumably thus allowing the flowers to support

better the weight of pollinating insects. If picked too early, the stem remains weak, and even though it may dry straight when hung upside down, the tip will always be liable to droop when subsequently used in an arrangement. The last-minute hardening of the stem makes a big difference to the final quality of the dried specimen.

Of the species detailed in this section, *Echinops* is the only one which must be harvested in bud. *Carthamus* and cardoons can be cut in bud or later in flower, according to the effect or colour which is required. Lavender, marjoram and thyme are best cut in bud or the very early stages of flowering and so have been included here.

Carthamus tinctorius
SAFFLOWER OR FALSE SAFFRON

Background
Carthamus is native to central Europe, central Asia and the Mediterranean. The bright orange flowers are used as a fabric dye – the Hebrew *Qarthami* and Arabic *Qurtom* mean 'to paint' or to 'colour'. The name 'false saffron' indicates its use as a poor (and cheaper) substitute for saffron and is sold as such in markets in the Middle East. These days, safflower is also grown commercially as a cut flower and for the production of oil from its seeds.

Uses for arranging
The flower is distinctive in autumnal or rustic displays. The sturdy, branching form and bright green buds give

structure and foliage colour in large open displays, tightly arranged baskets and formal topiary designs. It can be dyed a range of strong colours, such as terracotta, burgundy, blue and dark green and is thus especially valuable as a filler, providing a long-lasting background that helps to show off the focal flowers. Its natural green colour inevitably fades if exposed to bright light so it should only be used for short-term effect or in displays that are located away from direct light.

Cultivation
Carthamus is a fast growing annual, producing thistle-like flowering heads on strong, branched, woody stems about 75cm (30in) high. There are cream, yellow and orange varieties available, some of which have a more prickly head. There is also a taller

growing (1m/3ft high), non-prickly variety which flowers a week or two later, but which is selected commercially to be cut in bud. *Carthamus* can be sown direct as soon as the risk of frost is past and will be ready for cutting about three months later. Plants are best grown at close spacing – the competition encourages upright growth with fewer laterals and flowering is therefore more even.

Harvesting
If *Carthamus* is to be cut in green bud, a close watch needs to be kept on the plants as they approach flowering in mid-summer. If cut too early, the buds will tend to shrivel and be of no use. As soon as one plant displays the first hint of orange flower on its leading bud, the rest should be cut as soon as possible before they break bud too.

Drying
Because the buds are on the verge of bursting, it is necessary to ensure that they are dried quickly to prevent further development and that they are dried in the dark to retain their colour. If dried too slowly the buds will continue to develop and may start to burst open – the half-developed *Carthamus* is then neither one thing nor the other and its range of use will be restricted in floral displays.

To test dryness, break open a head – avoiding the prickles. The young flower developing inside should easily rub off from the base of the bud which should then snap and break easily. If the inside feels slightly oily or if the base of the bud where it joins the stem bends rather than snaps, then the specimen is not yet fully dry.

Cynara cardunculus
CARDOON

Background
Originating from Mediterranean regions, the cardoon is sometimes known as the Spanish artichoke. The name derives from the Greek *kynos* – meaning 'dog' – because the bracts around the flowering head resemble dogs' teeth.

Uses for arranging
The main value of cardoons is in the bold texture of the heads which, if closed, are ideal for use in wreaths or tight topiary trees. They are especially attractive when sprayed gold for festive decorations. The fully open purple flowers can form a dramatic display on their own (see page 84) or can contrast splendidly with grey eucalyptus and either white or lavender blue larkspur.

Cultivation
The cardoon is a hardy perennial, taller and more resilient than the artichoke. It grows best in good soil but will tolerate quite dry conditions. It can be grown from seed and produces a large 'rosette' of grey-green leaves, the stems of which – if blanched like celery – are edible. The leaves are surprisingly hardy in the winter and seem to survive frosts despite the stems' fleshiness. The purple, thistle-like flowers are produced in summer on a branched, woody stem that can grow to a height of 3m (9ft). As a garden plant, it is valuable for its height and for the colour and persistence of its foliage.

Harvesting
The cardoon can be cut for drying in mid-summer when in bud or in flower. On the branched stems, the leading buds develop into flower first and are gradually followed by the others. The fat buds can be individually cut on short stems or branches selected that have a mixture of open and closed heads. It is not advisable to wait until all the heads are in flower because the earliest ones will, by then, have begun to go over and turn brown, thus spoiling the overall effect.

When working intensively on a commercial scale with cardoons, some people have been known to develop an allergic reaction resulting in nose-bleeds or headaches – this may be as a result of the distinctive smell or the pollen. However, in a domestic situation it is rarely a problem.

Drying
The brown/green colour of the bracts, which may be tinged with burgundy, is retained well during and after drying. Flowers that have started to open will continue to develop during the drying process but the change is not as dramatic as with artichokes.

The drying process is slow because of the density of the heads, but needs to be thorough if they are to be stored. Dryness can be tested by carefully inserting a sharp knife into the underside of the head where it joins the stem. Any softness that remains is immediately apparent. Alternatively, the heads can be used fresh and allowed to dry in situ in a display.

Echinops sp.
GLOBE THISTLE

Background
The globe thistle originated in the Mediterranean regions and western Asia. The name *echinos* in Greek means 'hedgehog' - an appropriate description of the round, spiny flower-head.

Uses for arranging
The steely grey-blue, spherical flower-head is a glorious shape and texture to work with. It lends itself to 'English country garden' combinations with pink larkspur and red peonies (see the fireplace display on page 101) but it can also be used effectively on its own or with blue, grey or creamy tones, such as with *Gypsophila*, lavender and eucalyptus in the Chinese style vase on page 129. The heads are fragile and need to be handled with care. It is therefore advisable to use them during the latter stage of completing an arrangement to prevent accidental damage.

Cultivation
Echinops is a hardy perennial, growing to 1–1.5m (3–5ft) and preferring a good soil in a sunny location. It can be grown from seed or propagated by division. There are several garden varieties, but for drying choose the bluest. *E. bannaticus* is a good, neat, dark blue type. *E. ritro* has a larger head but is greyer and more liable to disintegrate with handling. The leaves are prone to infestation by aphids which can stunt growth and cause distortion – the problem can start early in the season before the flowers appear so be ready to take action!

(top to bottom) The stages of development of Echinops. *For drying, pick only at the first stage before the flower opens.*

Harvesting
Echinops must be harvested in bud. Once it starts to flower in early summer, the beautiful spherical shape is lost and the florets discolour and will readily be dislodged from the head if knocked. Precise timing is needed. If the bud is picked too early it will be small and relatively colourless and the stem will be too weak to support the head after drying. The bud must be allowed to develop to its full size, with as much blue colouring as possible. The ideal time to pick is one or two days before it would have come into flower – and experience is the only true guide to this. The leader stem flowers first, followed by the laterals over the space of several weeks. Longer-stemmed growth of the laterals can be encouraged if you wish by removing the leader bud early in the season.

Drying
Having picked the bud while on the verge of flowering, it is essential to prevent further development, so speedy drying is essential. Removal of the prickly leaves before drying makes subsequent handling easier. The dried heads must be handled with great care.

Lavandula
LAVENDER

Background
One of the most popular and versatile flowers, lavender is known throughout the world. It is a member of the Labiatae family which includes several other aromatic herbs such as sage and mint. Its strong aromatic qualities have long been used as an insect and moth repellent and in the past it was strewn on floors or carried in posies to disguise unpleasant smells. The commercial production of lavender oil, which began in France in the 17th century, promoted its use as a perfume though it was also recommended medicinally for its soothing and antiseptic properties. Lavender is currently much used in aromatherapy.

Uses in arranging
Apart from the scent, the deep blue flowers are delightful in any display of summer flowers. The heads are individually small so are best used grouped in clumps or sculpted into topiary shapes. Lavender combines well with roses, peonies and larkspur in 'country garden' styles but also looks very effective simply hanging in a bunch tied with ribbon or raffia.

Cultivation
The criteria for selecting varieties for use in lavender bags or pot-pourri will be based on scent not flower colour, but for use in arrangements it is important to grow the darkest purple types with growth habits that give good long stems, such as *Lavandula angustifolia* 'Hidcote' and 'Imperial Gem'.

Lavandula x *intermedia* 'Grosso' is the main commercial cultivar of lavandin, grown for oil production. Taller growing and strongly scented, the stems are sturdy but the heads tend to have a slightly more ragged look and are not such a dark blue. Careful handling is needed when dry as the flower-heads shed rather more readily than *L. angustifolia*.

All lavenders prefer dry, sunny locations and can tolerate poor, stony soils. As with many other aromatic herbs, these conditions positively benefit the oil production.

Harvesting
For decorative use, colour and sturdiness are the characteristics which dictate the harvesting stage. The dark blue colour is always strongest when the lavender is in full bud, just before it comes into flower, or when the first few flowers are opening and the stem has developed some woodiness at the tip. Keep a careful watch on the plants and start cutting as soon as the first flowers appear. It may be that certain patches in a bed of lavender may be ready before others, so cut selectively. The flowers themselves are always paler in colour than the buds and, on drying, can tinge grey or brown thus spoiling the overall effect. Also, the later the stage of development, the more readily the flowers will drop off the stem when they are dried and being handled.

If the lavender is required purely for its scent, the stems can be picked later in flower and, when dry, rubbed gently to remove the heads which can then be stored in the traditional way in muslin bags.

Drying
Lavender, being a woody plant, dries easily and quickly and advantage should be taken of its wonderful scent as it does so. Left to dry in wardrobes or airing cupboards it will deter moths and mice. The stems do not shrink noticeably during drying so the fresh-cut bunches can be tied with raffia or ribbon as charming decorative features.

Lavandula *sp. Try to pick as the first buds start to flower.*

Origanum vulgare
WILD MARJORAM

Background
Originating in Mediterranean regions, wild marjoram was valued for its medicinal properties – having preservative and antiseptic qualities – and was considered a remedy for poisons. It had religious and spiritual associations for the Greeks and Romans who wound it into bridal wreaths. It was also associated with funeral ceremonies; its presence on a grave signified the well-being of the departed. The aromatic oils were used for massage. In medieval times wild marjoram was used as a strewing herb in the house and for scenting water for washing.

The leaves have always been used in cooking, but these days it is the cultivated species which have the greatest culinary popularity – particularly *Origanum onites* (pot marjoram) and the low-growing annual *Origanum majorana* (sweet or knotted marjoram).

Uses in arranging
Apart from being a natural ingredient in herbal wreaths, the value of wild marjoram to a flower arranger lies in its dark pink colour which provides a wonderful contrast to the lighter pinks of larkspur, *Helichrysum* and peonies. Being compact in form and on a woody stem, it is easy to use and lends itself to small intricate work. It is especially useful for decorating hats, making corsages or hand-tied bouquets and, in keeping with its traditional associations, for binding into bridal headdresses.

Origanum vulgare. *Here the deep purple buds are just beginning to open into pink flower.*

Cultivation
Wild marjoram is a perennial herb which thrives and seeds readily in warm, dry conditions with light soil, growing to a height of 30–45cm (12–16in). In Europe it is native to areas of chalk grassland and flowers in early summer. The pink-flowering plants vary in the intensity of the colouring of the bracts. Always select the darkest for best effect. Some purchased seed may appear with white flowers and light green stems which, if picked early enough, are also useful.

Harvesting
The colour for which the marjoram is valuable comes not from the flower but the bracts or buds. As with the lavender, the flower itself is paler in colour and can tend to tinge brown during drying. The best quality is achieved by picking when the stems have turned woody, just before or as the first flowers are opening. Alternatively, it is possible to wait until the tiny pink flowers have gone over and dropped and to pick at the seed-pod stage. The colour should still be dark and the stems completely woody.

Drying
Marjoram is quick and easy to dry and can be hung alongside thyme and sage in a kitchen. If picked at the later stage it can be used direct in some displays once discoloured flower heads have been picked off. If you have only a small crop of marjoram in the garden, strip the leaves after picking and keep them separate for cooking.

Origanum majorana *has insignificant flowers but is very aromatic.*

Origanum majorana
SWEET OR KNOTTED MARJORAM, OREGANO

This low-growing half-hardy annual is aromatic and popular for culinary use. Germination can be erratic. It grows to 30cm (12in) in height with grey-green leaves and tiny white flowers formed in a knot. As a dried flower, its value lies in its scent and it is thus a good filler for the front of a basket arrangement or as an ingredient in kitchen displays or herb rings. It needs to be cropped in late bud or early flower, when the stems have started to turn woody but before the tiny white petals can turn brown. Hang it in the kitchen to dry and enjoy the herbal scent.

Thymus vulgaris
COMMON THYME

Thyme is a low-growing perennial, bearing tiny pink flowers in late spring. Its value (apart from its culinary use) is as a foreground filler in small arrangements or as an element in herbal wreaths. In colour it combines well with terracotta and is useful in themed garlands or picture panels as illustrated on page 103.

The picking stage is when in late bud or early flower. It dries easily, though needs to be in a location away from direct light to prevent colour loss. Be careful not to cut it too low to the ground as this may impair re-growth.

A flower picked in early bloom will not have reached its prime as a fresh specimen but there may be good reasons why, for drying, it should not be allowed to develop further:

1 Fleshy-stemmed flowers continue to open during drying. Unless they are deliberately picked early they will tend to over-mature during drying, causing petals to drop or the centre to 'blow' and turn to seed. Examples of this are *Helichrysum*, *Anaphalis* and *Ammobium.*

2 Large, dense flowers are slow to dry and so also continue to open during the drying process. If cut in early flower they will be in their prime when dry. Examples of this are artichokes, carline thistles and sunflowers.

3 Some varieties, such as peonies and cornflowers, naturally have a very short flowering period of only a few days, and so need to be 'caught' before they go over. Roses also cannot be cut in glorious full bloom because of likely petal drop.

4 With certain species, it is their background colour that is important. For instance, *Solidago* is valued for its fresh lime-green colouring which is lost when it is mature.

5 Varieties that have a succession of blooms on one stem, for instance, larkspur, *Liatris* and poker statice, need to be picked when the majority of the flowers are in their prime and before the earliest flowers have started to go over.

There are many varieties that fall into this category of being picked in early flower and they all need to be carefully monitored during the harvesting period. Flowering stems have to be selected individually as they come ready, so cropping is almost invariably spread over several weeks.

Ammobium alatum 'Grandiflorum'. *The bud on the right is at the correct stage for picking.*

Ammobium alatum 'Grandiflorum'
WINGED EVERLASTING

Background
The name comes from the Greek *ammos* meaning 'sand', and *bio* meaning 'to live', thus indicating that the plant thrives in light, dry soils. The word *alatum* means 'winged', referring to the distinctively winged stems. Originating in Australia it was introduced into Europe in the early 1800s as 'Winged Sandflower' and illustrated in catalogues as a variety specifically to be grown for drying.

Uses in arranging
In form like a tiny white strawflower, the flowers of *Ammobium* are individually formed on the end of long, winged stems. These readily re-absorb moisture and tend to droop easily after drying, even in low humidity. The flowers therefore need to be wired into small groups before being placed in a display. They are ideal for small, intricate displays, when they can be fixed using a glue gun, or for inclusion in densely packed formal basket arrangements.

Cultivation
Ammobium is a hardy annual which may over-winter in a mild climate. Because of its straggly form of growth it is best established in dense clumps in full sun and in light, free-draining conditions. The stems grow to a height of 60–70cm (24–28in) but do not usually require support.

Harvesting
The flowers appear in mid-summer and need to be cut selectively every two or three days, when the first ring of white petals have opened but before the daisy-like yellow centres are visible. If picked when in full flower the centre will dry discoloured. Bunches for drying are best cut short since the long stems are weak and have no value and their fleshiness will tend to slow down the drying process.

Drying
A warm, airy location is best to ensure quick drying. The bunches are fully dry when the stems snap easily. Because of their readiness to reabsorb moisture they are best stored hanging upside down until required.

Anaphalis margaritacea
PEARL EVERLASTING

Background
Anaphalis has origins in the temperate mountain regions of North America and North-east Asia. In the wild there are a number of species but the variety *margaritacea*, which means pearl, is the most popular in cultivation. Certain species were used medicinally by the North American Indians for treating lung complaints or eradicating poisons, or as a body oil. It may have been introduced into Europe by Elizabethan sailors returning to England from the New World at the end of the 16th century.

Uses in arranging
Anaphalis forms clusters of small, white flowers similar to *Ammobium* but borne in soft clusters on woolly stems. Individual clusters are delightful in small intricate work, but in larger displays they are best wired in groups to form areas of highlight. Their effect is to give a natural 'herbaceous border' look.

Cultivation
Anaphalis is a hardy perennial, forming a delightful trouble-free plant for the front of the herbaceous border. Once established, it spreads to form a neat clump about 45cm (18in) high, with grey foliage.

Harvesting
Flowering in mid-summer, it should be picked before the flowers are fully open as it goes to seed very quickly. It can be picked when still in bud, but at this stage the thin top leaves extend beyond the head and therefore may detract from its form. The young flowers are brighter in colour than the bud, but go dull as soon as the centres disintegrate into fluffy seed.

Drying
As with *Ammobium*, the stems are fleshy and not strong enough when dry to support the flower-heads, so bunch length should be kept short and the drying completed quickly to minimize flower development. Because the plant is grey and white it keeps well and does not lose colour readily either during drying or afterwards. Snap the lower stems to test dryness.

Carlina acaulis
CARLINE THISTLE

Background
Native to the short grassland of mountains in central Europe, the carline thistle is a protected species in some areas, but it can be purchased as seed.

Uses in arranging
A personal favourite, the carline thistle can be a magnificent focal flower. with its soft creamy/biscuit-coloured centre, surrounded by strong, thin, silvery petals. It is particularly useful as a neutral focal flower in blue colour schemes – there being no large natural blue dried flowers that can fulfil the role. It can be used to complement hydrangeas and is eyecatching in Christmas displays. (See the stone urn filled with carlines on page 87 and the table centre on page 137). The only drawback is its vicious prickles. Almost all parts of the plant, apart from the soft centres of the flowers, are spiky, and thick gardening gloves are required for handling. The green leaves immediately below the flower can be retained if required, but usually it is easier to remove all but the smallest top leaves. Inserting them into an arrangement while wearing thick gloves can be tricky;

however, the soft bristles at the centre of the flower are very resilient so the heads can be pushed firmly into place.

Cultivation
It is a stemless thistle in its natural habitat and grows happily on poor, thin alkaline soils. In better soil the flower stems may grow to 30cm (12in), which makes them a lot easier to handle and use. A hardy perennial, it can be grown from seed, forming a mass of prickly dark green leaves and flowering in its second year. The fleshy leaf stems are susceptible to winter slug damage.

Harvesting
Flowering in mid to late summer, they react to damp weather conditions, closing up at night and at the onset of rain. They can therefore only be picked in dry, sunny weather, preferably in the afternoon when they have opened sufficiently for its correct stage of development to be ascertained. They continue to develop during drying so they need to be picked when the inner circle of petals has opened to reveal the middle, but the petals have not progressed much further than a 90–135° angle to the centre. By the time the head is dry, the petals will have opened.

Centaurea cyanus. *Ideally cornflowers should be picked one day earlier than this full-flowering stage.*

Drying
The stems are strong so the flowers do not necessarily need to be hung up to dry but care must be taken to ensure that the silvery petals are not bent or creased during drying or storage. Drying in the dark is advisable if leaf colour is to be retained. If a flower-head has been picked late and has started to go to seed by the time it is dry, the dark seeds can be carefully pulled out to retain the cream colour of the centre. Test dryness where the flower head joins the stem.

Centaurea cyanus
CORNFLOWER

Background
A traditional European flower of meadow grassland, the glorious blue cornflower (*kyanos* in Greek means 'dark blue') has a surprisingly tough stem and, in the days of hand-reaping of corn, was known as 'hurt sickle' because of its blunting effect. It has always been a popular cottage garden flower and is often chosen for wedding bouquets. Its thin, strong, pliable stem made it popular in the past for weaving into garlands.

Uses in arranging
When dried, the cornflower is fragile to use but well worth it because of its intensity of colour. Individually the heads stand out well in delicate work (see the bridesmaids' circlets and posy on page 142) and if wired together in groups are useful in densely packed arrangements (see the Chinese vase on page 129).

Carlina acaulis. *The topmost flower is at the ideal picking stage.*

Cultivation
The cornflower is a half-hardy annual, easily grown from seed and requiring full sun. Since it can grow up to 60cm (24in) and requires support to ensure straight upright stems, it is best sown in small blocks or short rows supported by netting. A small area can produce a large quantity of flowers which are time-consuming to pick and need regular attention, so beware of over-enthusiasm when sowing. Although available in white, pink, mauve or purple,

it is the double-flowered, darkest blue one that is the best to grow for drying. If sown in early spring it will be ready to crop about three months later.

Harvesting
The cornflower matures and fades within a few days of breaking bud, so needs to be picked when half open, before the centre stamens are visible. Cropping can continue over several weeks and needs to be done ideally on a daily basis, or at least every other day. If

left longer than this, the flowers will rapidly start to pale in colour and be of no use. If bad weather causes delays it is a good idea to cut and discard all such heads to make future selection easier.

Drying
Tie with small rubber bands in bunches of ten or twenty heads. Drying must be fast or the colours will fade and the heads will tend to disintegrate. Store in layers separated by paper to prevent the heads becoming tangled.

Cynara scolymus
ARTICHOKE

Background
The artichoke is related to the cardoon and has been developed commercially for its large edible head. It grows most readily in warm, temperate regions such as France and Spain but, is easily killed off in the colder winters of northern Europe. The leaves are more finely cut than the cardoon and the artichoke flowers form on single or simply branched stems, at a height of about 1–1.5m (3–5ft).

Uses for arranging
The closed buds can be used in the same way as cardoons – as focal, sculptural elements in a design and can be sprayed gold to good effect. The large

Cynara scolymus. *If cut when first showing colour, it will open into full flower during drying.*

open flowers which, on a mature plant can measure up to 25cm (10in) across, are glorious features in big displays but are also delightful just on their own.

Cultivation
The large single seeds should be sown, 60cm (24in) or more apart, in the late spring and may produce a small crop of heads in the early autumn of their first year. In subsequent years, much larger heads will develop and flower during the summer months. To prevent damage from winter frosts the plants should be protected; but, be warned – too cosy a winter microclimate may result in damage from slugs attracted to the fleshy stems.

Harvesting
The closed buds can be cut at the edible stage, and dried. If wishing to dry the flowering heads it is necessary to cut them one stage ahead of how they should look. To obtain full flowering colour, cut them when the first tuft of mauve flower is beginning to show. If cut when fully open, the flower will go to seed while drying but any discoloured florets can be pulled out to reveal the biscuit-coloured seed tufts. In full colour the artichoke is glorious but it is equally useful for its size and form when it is this later neutral colour.

Drying
Artichokes are dense and take a long time to dry but all they need is warmth. They can hang upside down or be supported upright – but, before bringing them inside to dry, give the heads a good shake to remove resident earwigs. Dryness can be tested with a sharp knife, as for cardoons (see page 50).

Delphinium consolida. *This stem still has a couple of buds at the top but the flowers at the base have not started to go to seed.*

Delphinium consolida
LARKSPUR

Background
This is the annual larkspur, one of a number of species native to the Mediterranean area and naturalized in parts of Asia. It was introduced into England in the second half of the 16th century and since then has become synonymous with the English country garden. Its name comes from the Greek *delphin* because of a supposed resemblance to dolphins' heads. *Consolida* means 'joined in one' which is a reference to the way the flowers are densely packed on the spike.

Uses in arranging
One of the most popular dried flower varieties, larkspur's versatility is partly due to its useful range of bright colours – white, light blue, lavender blue, dark blue, and a range of pinks. The tall spires provide excellent visual structure to big displays, giving strength and direction, while the shorter laterals are equally useful in smaller arrangements, especially long, low table centres. Petal colours last well, particularly the dark blue, and colour loss through age may only be noticeable on the stems and young buds.

Cultivation
Double-flowered varieties, on which the flowers are densely packed up the spike, give the best effect when dried. 'Blue Spire' is an excellent dark blue and, of the various pink colours available, 'Salmon Beauty' is strong and long-lasting. In temperate climates, larkspur should be direct-sown in the autumn to flower in early summer, or spring-sown to flower in mid-summer. It likes full sunshine and a free-draining soil and grows best in blocks or rows when the leader stems are encouraged to be tall (approximately 1m/3ft high) and straight. It can be susceptible to mildew.

Harvesting
Invariably the dark blue variety flowers first, followed by the pink and white. Cropping needs to be selective, cutting the stems on which about 90 percent of the flower buds have opened. In a display, it is the top part of the spike that will be seen, so it needs to have as much flower colour on it as possible. However, if left to open fully to the tip, there is the risk that the lowest flowers will have started to go to seed (or will over-mature during drying), resulting in petal drop. The white larkspur can be cropped at a slightly earlier stage (80 percent in flower), since the creamy-green buds are, themselves, very attractive.

Because larkspur is often used as a tall background flower in displays, its length is important. Do not, however, cut stems longer than you actually need because this limits the potential growth of lateral shoots which, even if they are only 30cm (12in) long, are valuable. Cropping of these laterals can extend the harvesting period by several weeks.

Drying
The greenness of the stem and bud-tips is important to the 'fresh' look of the dried flower, so fast drying in the dark is necessary to achieve the best quality. Larkspur is fully dry when the thickest stems snap easily. If the flowers have been picked a little late or dried too slowly and some of the petals drop, collect them! Larkspur petals are excellent as wedding confetti or a colourful ingredient in pot-pourri.

Delphinium elatum
DELPHINIUM

The perennial delphinium, much taller than its annual cousin, can be dried equally successfully. It is rarely available commercially as a dried flower, being expensive to produce and too big to package effectively, so is an ideal candidate for garden production for use in big pedestal displays. Select varieties with double flowers, closely packed on the stem and pick when the tip of the spike has become firm, but before the lower flowers have over-matured.

Dianthus barbatus. *Select the darker heads for drying.*

Dianthus barbatus
SWEET WILLIAM

Background
A member of the carnation family, the name *Dianthus* means 'divine flower' (*Dios* is 'god' and *anthos* a 'flower'). The individual florets of Sweet William, are packed together to form a flat-topped flower-head.

Uses in arranging
Although available as a fresh-cut flower in season, Sweet William is rarely available commercially as a dried flower. Grown in the garden, it can make a useful contribution as an unusual background filler in arrangements, to show off light pink larkspur, *Helichrysum* or roses.

Helianthus annuus
SUNFLOWER

Background
It is thought that in England the name sunflower was originally applied to the marigold, but it is now the common name of the giant flower which originated in Peru and Mexico (where it was venerated by the sun-worshipping Aztecs) and was introduced into Europe in the 16th century. The sunflower rapidly gained popularity as an agricultural crop throughout Europe and North America because of the versatility of its different parts for cattle feed, paper-making and dyeing. But its most significant product was the oil from the seeds. Sunflower oil is now widely available for culinary use as well as being a lubricant and a constituent of paint. The giant sunflower, popular as a garden plant, can grow to 3–4m (9–12ft), but the agricultural variety is manageably shorter, being 1.5–2m (5-6ft) high.

Cultivation
A sturdy and reliable biennial growing to about 40cm (16in), seeds should be sown outdoors in late spring and can be transplanted ready for flowering a year later. Flower colours can be crimson red, dark pink, white or variegated. The dark colours tend to have darker coloured heads overall and are therefore better at providing contrast and holding colour longer than the lighter flowering varieties. The white-flowered variety can, however, be very attractive when freshly dried, though tends to fade rapidly.

Harvesting and drying
Crop when in early flower (or late bud) and dry as quickly as possible, in the dark.

Helianthus annuus *must be picked before the petals have opened fully.*

Uses in arranging
There are two useful varieties, the traditional black-centred flower with its golden halo, and the fully double flower, densely packed with yellow petals. Bold and dramatic in form, both are eyecatching either in single variety displays (see page 41) or in combination with grasses and rustic autumnal colours. The giant sunflower may be too massive for most displays and is very difficult to dry successfully at home – either distorting badly in shape or turning to seed – but its large, dark, disc-shaped seed head can offer an interesting form and texture for use with exotic sculptural shapes.

Cultivation
Select either the double *Helianthus* (perhaps 'Sungold') or the short-growing form of the single, black-centred *H. annuus* (maybe 'Sunrich Orange'), and sow in full sun in the spring, to flower in late summer. Remember that the sunflower always turns to the sun and so plant it where you can enjoy its face, not the back of its head! Generally, the agricultural varieties are sturdy and do not need staking, though are occasionally susceptible to wind-blow in exposed areas.

The black-centred sunflowers usually flower singly on a stem, whereas the double-flowered varieties produce more laterals shoots. One problem with these doubles is that the length of the lateral stems is annoyingly short. This can be remedied by removing the leader bud and so encouraging the laterals to grow longer.

Harvesting
If the heads are wet when picked, the petals will fade and discolour during drying, so only crop in dry, sunny weather. Because sunflowers are large and dense, they take a long time to dry and so must be picked in early flower. The petals that surround the centre of the black sunflower are initially all bent in towards the middle. Over several days, the petals open out until, in full flower, they have progressed through 180°. To prevent the head going to seed during the drying process, it is essential to pick the flowers when the petals have opened to only a 90–120° angle to the black centre.

The double sunflowers need to be picked when the centre petals are still tightly packed and before the outer petals have started to reflex back. If picked any later, the petals tend not to hold on to the head when dried and are easily dislodged.

Drying
Sunflowers must be dried fast, with heat and rapid air movement. Even in commercial kilns they can take ten to fourteen days to dry fully. The large lower leaves should be stripped off and the stems banded in pairs and hung upside down. Large heads tend to twist in shape as they shrink during drying but this can add to their character.

The part which indicates dryness is the top of the stem immediately beneath the head. Sometimes the stem can feel superficially dry but, if it is taken out of the heat and left for a while, more moisture may be drawn out from the head to soften it again. Do not be caught out, as the flower will rapidly go mouldy if packed too soon.

Helichrysum bracteatum monstrosum
STRAWFLOWER

Background
The *Helichrysum* family comprises annuals, perennials and shrubs, all of which originated from Australia and South Africa. They were introduced into Europe in the late 18th and early 19th centuries and by the mid-19th century the annual double flowering *H. bracteatum* was featuring in plant catalogues specifically for drying, along with other immortelles – *Rhodanthe*, *Acroclineum* (often now referred to as *Helipterum*), *Ammobium*, statice and *Xeranthemum* – all of which feature stiff papery petals. Other *Helichrysum* forms, such as the shrubby *H. italicum* can also be dried but are not grown specifically for this purpose.

Uses in arranging
The Greek name *helios* meaning 'the sun' and *chrusos* meaning 'gold' belies the wide range of colours that the strawflower provides. No other dried flower equals it for range and versatility – light pink, dark pink, purple, scarlet, orange, salmon, gold, lemon and cream. Each lends itself to a different use. The cream links well with blue schemes, the purple provides fabulous depth to lighter pinks, the lemon is delightful in springtime especially combined with light blues, the orange lends itself to autumnal colourings along with *Carthamus* and natural grasses, and the pinks link well with lavender, peonies and roses. The other asset of the *Helichrysum* is its colour retention; even over the space of a couple of years it seems only to be dulled by dust!

The drawback of the plant is that its stem is very fleshy, causing the heads to continue to open during the drying process and the resultant stems to be brittle and too weak to support the head. A solution in the past was to pick only the heads and stick or spike them on to wires to dry. This resulted in the flowers being used individually, dotted around in arrangements, creating the all too common pincushion effect (often in combination with sea lavender *Limonium dumosum*). This unnatural presentation, combined with the fact that the home-grown flowers were invariably picked too late and dried too slowly so had overblown, has tended to give the poor *Helichrysum* a very down-market image.

Correctly picked, dried in its prime and appropriately grouped in arrangements it is an extremely valuable element in the florist's palette – as witnessed by its regular occurrence throughout this book.

Cultivation
Helichrysum bracteatum monstrosum is a half-hardy annual preferring full sun and a well-drained soil. It is advisable to select specific colours, rather than buy mixed seed – which always emerges with a predominance of the colours you require least. Dark pink and salmon are the two of the most useful ones. Sow the seed in early spring after the last frosts, or germinate under glass and transplant out in late spring. Because the flowers need to be picked before they are open, they are never eyecatching in a flower garden and are best cultivated in a separate plot. Flowering starts in mid-summer and, with good nutrient and water supply, continues productively until the autumn frosts. Lateral growth can be encouraged by removal of the primary bud early in the season. The succulent stem can sometimes attract snails and the leaves may be susceptible to mildew.

Harvesting
The flowers close up overnight and in damp weather, so picking can only be done at dry, sunny times. The picking stage is crucial and needs to be done selectively, inspecting the crop every two or three days. The outer ring of petals should be open but the rest still forming a pointed bud. Picked at this stage, the other petals will open to full effect, giving maximum colour, without revealing the centre of the flower. Stems should not be cut any longer than necessary, to allow maximum regrowth.

Sometimes in continued wet weather, or later in the season, the flower will mature inside while the petals remain closed over it. A dark hole in the centre of the bud indicates that this has happened, and these flowers will 'blow' as soon as they are dried. Commercially, quality is judged on the size and stage of opening of the flowers, and bunches should not contain more than a few fully open heads. The one exception is the purple variant on which the creamy colour of the centre can be an attractive contrast to the darkness of the surrounding petals.

Helichrysum bud at the perfect stage for picking.

Liatris spicata which flowers from the top down.

Drying
Bunches should be small and bound tightly with rubber bands since shrinkage of the stems is significant. They should be hung upside down and dried as fast as possible to minimize flower development. In commercial kilns, drying takes five to seven days. To test dryness, snap stems at the centre of a bunch, under the rubber band. If bone dry, the stems are very brittle and heads can easily break off, so handle dried bunches with care and keep broken heads for glue-gun work or potpourri. In a damp atmosphere, moisture will readily be reabsorbed, causing the stems to become weak and floppy, unable to support the weight of the flower.

Helichrysum flowers have a distinctive scent and are susceptible to moth damage. They should be dried in a moth-free environment (using insect repellents if necessary) and stored in sealed boxes containing mothballs.

Liatris spicata
GAY FEATHERS

Native to North America, *Liatris* is a herbaceous perennial, not commercially grown for drying, but nevertheless an interesting flower to use from the garden because of its bright purple colour and distinctive form. It likes full sun and tolerates poor, light soils but cannot stand competition. It will flower best (with spikes up to 75cm/30in) in a rich soil.

Unlike most flowers, which open progressively from the bottom of a flowering spike (such as larkspur), *Liatris* starts to open from the top. This is helpful in flower arranging since it is the top of the spike which is always seen. The stem is quite woody, so its form does not change much during drying and it can be dried upright. The picking stage is determined by allowing as many flowers as possible to open before the top flowers start to mature. Dry quickly to prevent it going to seed.

(top row, left to right) The many colours of Helichrysum: *lemon, gold, orange, scarlet, purple, salmon, dark pink, silver rose, cream.*
(centre stems, left to right) Xeranthemum annuum, Helichrysum bracteatum monstrosum, Carlina acaulis, Solidago canadensis, Anaphalis margaritacea, Liatris spicata, Ammobium alatum *'Grandiflorum'.*
(cluster of heads, bottom left) Two heads of Helianthus annuus *with the double-flowered* Helianthus *'Sungold'.*
(bottom row of heads, left to right) The development of Helichrysum *heads during drying. Each will open during drying to the stage one or two further to the right. The second and third specimen are at the correct stage for picking.*

Limonium suworowii
POKER STATICE

Most members of this family are picked in full flower (see page 68), but the extraordinary *L. suworowii* (a Russian name) is the exception. The tiny flowers are densely packed up a tall, thin, wavy, mauve-pink spire. Pick when the tip of the spike is beginning to feel firm and most of the flowers have opened but the top is still in dark pink bud. Unusual and delicate, the poker statice is very pretty in bouquets (see the wedding bouquet on page 141).

Limonium suworowii.

Paeonia officinalis and P. lactiflora
PEONY

Background
The peony is named after the physician of ancient Greece, Paeon, who reputedly first used its medicinal properties to treat the Olympian gods. The powdered roots were thought to cure nervous conditions. Found throughout Europe, Asia, China and North West America, the peony is one of the oldest flowers in cultivation and has always been especially popular in oriental art. It is a symbol of good fortune and a protector against evil spirits.

Cultivation
A herbaceous perennial, the best peonies for drying are the large, double-flowered heads, especially the varieties 'Sarah Bernhardt' (light pink), 'Monsieur Jules Elie' (dark pink), 'Duchesse de Nemours' (cream) and 'Rubra plena' (an old-fashioned dark red). Of the single-flowered types, 'Bowl of Beauty' is very striking with its bright creamy yellow centre surrounded by dark pink petals.

Peonies will thrive in sun or light shade, preferring a deep rich soil. They will grow from seed but, since they take several years to flower, establishment from plants is advisable. The buds are susceptible to late frosts so plants should be located in a sheltered spot.

Harvesting
Once a peony bud has opened, it develops very fast and in less than a week can have matured and begun to drop its petals. For drying it is crucial to pick heads when they have started to open and

Uses in arranging
Being such a glorious flower in full bloom, picking it to dry seems sacrilegious. Consolation can, however, be sought in the fact that in its fresh state it can only be enjoyed for a few days, whereas when dried its glory will last for months!

Peonies add a classic elegance to any arrangement, and are often mistaken for old-fashioned roses. They combine well with *Gypsophila*, hydrangeas and larkspur, and are excellent focal flowers for wedding bouquets, garlands and big arrangements. The dark pink and red blooms hold their colour well, though the cream varieties turn an antique parchment colour over time and the light pink ones go paler.

Paeonia 'Sarah Bernhardt'. Pick just before the petals start to curve. back..

the head is as large as possible, but before the outer petals have reflexed back. With the double flowers, there will still be some petals in the centre that have not yet unfurled. If the young seedpods are visible, the bloom has opened too far and the petals will drop during drying. The faster the drying facilities, the later the flower can be picked, so be prepared to learn by trial and error.

Be careful if buying peonies for drying that have been cut in tight bud for the fresh-flower market. They may also have been cold-stored to slow their development and Botrytis rot can sometimes affect these heads, destroying them before they open.

Drying
Remove the lower leaves and air-dry upside down in a warm, dark place. High heat or a hot, humid atmosphere will cause browning of petals on the cream and light pink varieties. The flowers, enormous when fresh, will shrink to less than half their original size. They need to be bone dry for storage and some of the petals will look crumpled or be distorted from pressing against others in the bunch. To rectify this before placing blooms in a display, hold the heads over a steaming kettle – the petals will soften and expand, and can then be gently teased back into shape.

Drying in silica crystals maintains a fuller shape and is the preferred method of drying for small quantities. See page 46 and page 104 for

fuller details of this method and the illustration of a display using silica-dried peonies.

Peonies, especially the 'Sarah Bernhardt' and 'Duchesse de Nemours' varieties which have a strong scent, are susceptible to moth damage. It is advisable to hang moth repellent near them during drying and to store them in sealed boxes in a dry location.

(left to right) Delphinium consolida, Centaurea cyanus, Limonium suworowii, Paeonia 'Sarah Bernhardt', Paeonia 'Monsieur Jules Elie', Delphinium consolida, Rosa 'Mercedes', Dianthus barbatus.

Rosa sp.
ROSES

Background
The rose appears throughout the history of many countries in the northern hemisphere and features wherever gardens are mentioned. The range of varieties now available is immense – both for the garden and as commercially grown cut flowers.

Uses in arranging
Roses will always be important flowers in an arrangement, adding class and refinement. The large double blooms, if silica-dried, resemble peonies and can be used to fill elegant bowls as table-centre displays or be arranged in the style of the old Dutch flower paintings in classical urns of mixed species, perhaps combined with hydrangeas and trailing *Amaranthus*. Topiary trees can be made of densely packed flowers or, for an informal look, the heads can be given false stems (the wire being concealed with moss) and 'rambling roses' created to twine around furniture or over mirrors (see the chair on the endpiece'). The old Apothecary's Rose – *Rosa gallica officinalis* – was always much prized for its perfume and the dried petals can be strewn among clothes and linen or used in pot-pourri. The small, double spray roses dry well and are delightful in posies.

Cultivation
If selecting garden rose varieties specifically for their drying qualities, choose the large double-flowered ones. Single-flowered types are probably best pressed or dried for their petals.

Buying or harvesting
Rules for harvesting are similar to peonies. Pick before the flowers are fully open and before the outer petals have curved back. With roses, whether from the garden or the flower market, it is necessary to experiment to ascertain which varieties will hold their colour best. Generally, colours that are dark or strong when fresh are more successful because they intensify when dried whereas lighter colours tend to go pale and quickly look faded. A bright orange-red rose will dry to a strong mid-red, whereas a mid-red fresh rose turns to a deep velvet red.

If drying commercially grown roses, choose types with flat-topped buds and a dense bowl of petals. Pointed bud types may not be so full of petals and will therefore not hold their shape so well when dried. The following glasshouse-grown varieties have a proven track record - 'Jaguar' (dark red), 'Mercedes' (bright red), 'Europa' (dark pink), 'Kiss' (mid-pink), 'Gerdo' (peach) and 'Golden Time' (yellow). Having been cut in bud for market, the stems need to be trimmed again and bunches stood in water to allow the heads to open before being hung to dry.

Drying
Dry by hanging the bunches upside-down in the dark. The more open a bloom is when it is picked, the faster it needs to be dried to prevent petals from dropping; this applies particularly to garden roses. You may find that some varieties drop their petals more readily than others – if so, you will have the basis of a new pot-pourri.

Sometimes bought roses have been out of water too long, and the air-locks in the stems cause the heads to droop. Rather than consigning them to an early fate on the compost heap or in the dustbin, hang them up to dry. The flowers may have only just started to open but they will dry successfully and still be decorating your home months later.

As with peonies, silica-drying is more effective in maintaining the head size than air-drying and is an especially useful method for preserving the large blooms of old-fashioned English roses.

Store dried roses in sealed boxes, with mothballs to deter insects.

English Rose 'Evelyn', showing petals densely packed and ideal for drying.

Solidago canadensis. *Pick just as the first flowers begin to open.*

Solidago sp.
GOLDEN ROD

Background
The name *Solidago* comes from the plant's healing properties, meaning to join or make whole. Found in Europe, the Middle East, North America and Canada, it is a deciduous perennial that grows up to 2m (6ft) high, according to the variety. It is similar to *Solidaster* which is greenhouse-grown for the floristry trade.

Uses in arranging
Solidago is purely a filler, and its value lies in the lime-green/yellow colour of its buds and young flowers. Used in groups of stems alongside pinks and blues, it provides a delightful freshness to a display, though it is prone to fade after a while.

Cultivation
Solidago canadensis is a useful strong yellow variety, growing to 60cm (24in) in sun or light shade and tolerating poor, dry soils.

Harvesting
The yellow plumes are a mass of tiny flowers which open and turn to fluffy seed very quickly. The most useful stage for drying is as the first flowers begin to open.

Drying
The stem is woody, so drying is easy, but the process needs to be quick to retain the greenness of the leaves and young buds and to prevent the flowers going to seed.

These flowers can generally be picked when they are in their prime as fresh flowers, when their colour is at its best. Many of the woodier plant types fall into this category. Lack of moisture ensures that the flowers do not continue to develop during drying, but hold their form. Many of these varieties have a long flowering period and the exact timing of picking is not so crucial as with the earlier stages detailed on the previous pages. Drying is usually quick and easy. The *Achillea* and *Limonium* families feature strongly here.

Achillea filipendulina GOLDEN YARROW

Background
Achillea filipendulina originated in the Caucasus but is now a familiar plant in the herbaceous border with its flat-topped yellow heads. The family name derives from the Greek hero Achilles who used it to heal his soldiers' wounds.

Achillea filipendulina.

Uses in arranging
The golden yarrow has always been popular because it dries well, is sturdy and easy to handle, and holds its colour. Its bold circles of yellow are excellent when used full-face in compact displays, or when viewed side-on on the perimeter of larger, looser arrangements. The varieties 'Gold Plate' and 'Cloth of Gold' are the strongest golden yellow, whereas 'Moonshine' has a more subtle and lemony colour with a soft greyness to its stems and leaves.

Cultivation
The golden yarrows are hardy perennials, though 'Moonshine' can be more tender. They are tolerant of most soil conditions and prefer full sun. Growing to 1.5m (5ft) or higher, they are excellent at the back of a border where their long summer flowering period can be enjoyed.

Harvesting
If cut too early, the florets in the flower-head curl in and the impact of the colour is lost. The florets need to be fully open and picking delayed as long as possible before the blooms start to discolour. There is a useful 'thumb test' – as the flower-head is developing it feels soft and spongy in the middle and it is possible to see light through it. At maturity, the centre of the head, if gently pressed with the thumb, feels firm, the colour is dense, and the shape when viewed from the side has changed from concave to slightly convex.
   When picking, do not discard stems that have grown contorted because of light conditions – they can have great artistic value.

Drying
The leaves have no value so can can be stripped before drying to prevent them crumbling later. *A. filipendulina* dries quickly and easily.
   Experience in commercial production has suggested that the handling of large quantities of *A. filipendulina* requires a well-ventilated space if headaches and sneezing are to be avoided. It can also be a skin irritant.

Achillea millefolium 'Cerise Queen'.

Achillea millefolium COMMON YARROW

Background
In past times the common yarrow was called the military herb *Herba militaris*, Soldier's woundwort and Knights' Milfoil because of its use as a vulnerary – to stem the flow of blood and heal flesh wounds. The name of the common yarrow, with its flat-topped white or pale pink flowers, comes from the Anglo-Saxon *gearwe* and the Dutch *yerw*. Its Latin name *Achillea millefolium* means 'thousand leaves', referring to its feathery leaf form. Native to Europe and the Caucasus, it frequents road verges and is a persistent weed of lawns.

Uses in arranging
The native yarrow has two popular cultivars: 'Cerise Queen' (mid to dark pink) and 'Summer Pastels' (peach shades). These both offer subtle and useful colours as background fillers in basket arrangements, garlands or bouquets. The heads are softer in form than the golden yarrow and react unfavourably to a damp atmosphere.

Cultivation
Achillea millefolium is a reliable perennial of neat and compact form, growing to 60–75cm (24–30in). It spreads readily from seed.

Harvesting
The flower never attains the firmness of the golden yarrow but the rule is nevertheless to pick it when the individual florets have opened to their maximum. See above.

Drying
Being woody, the bunches dry quickly hanging upside down. Colours always become more muted during drying.

Achillea ptarmica 'The Pearl' SNEEZEWORT

Background
This *Achillea* has white flowers grouped at the top of thin, woody stems. It is like a double form of the herb feverfew (*Tanacetum parthenium*). The Greek word *ptarmicos* means 'sneezing' and the powdered, dried flowers were once used as an ingredient in snuff.

Uses in arranging
Being bright white and with strong stems, the flowers are versatile for use in displays, garlands, bouquets or delicate posies. Loose heads can be added to pot-pourri.

Cultivation
It is important to acquire a variety with fully double flowers. It can be grown from cuttings and, once established, will spread rapidly to form a large clump, flowering in early to mid-summer on stems that are about 1m (3ft) high. The plant is susceptible to mildew and may need preventative spraying during the growing season.

Harvesting
As with golden yarrow, 'The Pearl' takes a long time to reach the correct picking stage. The flowers need to be fully open and as white as possible. Harvesting should be in dry weather because wet flowers may discolour during drying.

Drying
Drying is quick and easy, but too high a temperature may cause the flowers to brown. Hang upside-down.

Agastache sp.
AGASTACHE

Agastache is a half-hardy perennial in the Hyssop family, and known for its strong scent. The most useful variety for drying is *A. urticifolia* 'Alba' which has a white flower, or the blue 'Coerulea'. Both have a mint-like growth form with tall flower spikes up to 70cm (28in) high on strong, branched woody stems. *Agastache* needs to be picked when the flower spike is firm to the tip but before the flowers can start to discolour. Dry with the bunches hanging vertically or the flower tips may droop and remain bent. The scented leaves are useful in pot-pourri.

Alchemilla mollis
LADY'S MANTLE

Alchemilla is a deciduous perennial native to northern Europe and Asia, North America and Canada. A delightful front-of-border plant, with its lime-green leaves and delicate flower sprays, the *Alchemilla* was valued by early chemists (alchemists) who collected the dew from its soft, hairy leaves. The scalloped leaves resemble a lady's shawl or mantle and it is therefore associated with the Virgin Mary.

The value of *Alchemilla* in arranging is its delicate form (especially useful in corsages and posies) as well as its fresh green colour. For best effect, it needs to be picked when the tiny flowers have just opened fully, and then dried quickly in the dark.

(left to right) Achillea filipendulina, Amaranthus paniculatus, Limonium dumosum, Achillea *'Moonshine'*, Limonium sinuatum, Achillea ptarmica *'The Pearl'*.

Amaranthus caudatus *in early flower.*

Amaranthus paniculatus, A. caudatus
LOVE-LIES-BLEEDING

Background
Amaranthus comes from the Greek and means 'not fading' or 'unwithering' and is therefore associated with images of immortality. However, there are also connections with the Latin *amor* meaning 'love', hence the common name of Love-lies-bleeding for the red trailing variety. The word *caudatus* means 'tailed' (describing a long tasselled form) and *paniculatus* refers to a broad upright flower panicle. This latter form is thought to have originated in the tropics and was introduced into Europe in the 16–17th century.

Uses in arranging
The long, trailing tassels of *A. caudatus* are fabulous in pedestal or tall urn displays or for hanging baskets and swags. The upright *A. paniculatus* is a useful filler in basket arrangements and the red form is especially valuable for its appropriately seasonal colour at Christmas.

Cultivation
Both the upright and trailing forms are available from seed with dark burgundy red or bright green forms. They are hardy annuals, flowering in late summer and requiring a rich, well-irrigated soil. *A. paniculatus* grows to 70cm (28in) in height but *A. caudatus* can reach over 1m (3ft) before then curving over. Both are susceptible to a rust disease on the leaves, but this does not detract from the quality of the flowers.

Harvesting
The panicles consist of tiny massed flowers. Maturity can only be detected by the overall intensity of colour and the presence of the yellow stamens. With the upright form, *A. paniculatus*, it is important that the top of the panicle has developed a firm stem and is not floppy. Immature flower-heads will wilt and droop as soon as they are picked whereas the mature ones will hold their form better. This characteristic is important in their final use, since it is their rigid uprightness which is a required characteristic. If picked too late, colour deteriorates and the head can disintegrate. The picking stage on the trailing form is not so critical.

The pollen of *Amaranthus* can cause itchiness to the skin during picking and when handling after drying.

Drying
Both types should be dried quickly in the dark. *A. paniculatus* must be dried upside down. Long *A. caudatus* can be hung upside down or the main stem laid flat and the flowering part allowed to trail. Gently curl it round into a box for storage.

The lower stems are thick and tough when dry. Test dryness by snapping the thickest part. Store and display *Amaranthus* in a dry atmosphere to prevent the upright panicles from drooping.

Carthamus tinctorius
SAFFLOWER

For background and cultivation, see the notes on *Carthamus* on page 50. *Carthamus* is one of the few varieties for which there is a choice of picking stages. It is cut in bud for use as a green filler, but can also be cut when in full bloom for its cream, yellow or bright orange flower-heads. The orange colour is the most popular and is very useful for terracotta or autumnal colour schemes or with green grasses.

Harvesting
Carthamus blooms in mid-summer. The flowers are borne singly on branched stems. The terminal bud opens first. Flowering in hot, dry weather is fast and even, which makes cropping easy since the aim is to pick when as many heads as possible are in their prime with maximum colour. Unfortunately, in dull, wet conditions some flowers start to die off before others have opened.

Drying
The dramatic effect of the flower is due to the contrast of its colour against the greenness of the calyx and leaves. It must therefore be dried quickly and in the dark to retain the freshness of its look. Test dryness by cutting a head in half, and rubbing off the developing seeds. If they can be easily dispersed, and the base of the head from which they are growing can be snapped, the head is dry. If the seeds are difficult to remove, and the base is supple, more drying is needed. Store in the dark and, for longevity, only use in arrangements that are not exposed to direct light.

Centaurea macrocephala
GIANT KNAPWEED

The giant knapweed is a reliable deciduous perennial, related to the cornflower, and growing to over 1m (3ft) high. It blooms in late spring with each stem having a large, single, bright yellow, thistle-like flower. Sturdy and straight, the flower combines well with grasses in tall rustic displays. The bloom should be picked as it approaches full flower, but before the outer petals start to curve outwards around the cup of feathery sepals. It is necessary to guard against moth damage during drying and storage.

Later in the season when the seeds have been produced, the remaining brown 'cup' can be used as an interesting shape in autumnal arrangements.

Centaurea macrocephala. *Ideally pick a day before this full flowering stage.*

Craspedia globosa
DRUMSTICK

Background
A native of Australia, 'drumstick' accurately describes the striking appearance of this flower – a tightly-packed ball of tiny florets at the end of a slim, strong, grey stem.

Uses in arranging
The flower provides distinctive and unusual points of interest in a display and is popular for its longevity both as a fresh and a dried flower.

Cultivation
Craspedia is a tender annual/biennial. The flowers grow to 75cm (30in) high over a rosette of thin grey leaves. Support may be needed on a rich soil. The plant is not competitive and, even if it survives a first winter outdoors, it will die off in the second. Seeds need to be sown under glass, pricked out after about five weeks and transplanted later when there is no danger of frost. Each plant only produces a few flowers, but it is nevertheless a worthwhile plant to grow at home since it is always expensive to buy.

Harvesting
Cut selectively in mid to late summer when the florets have fully opened to give a strong yellow colour but before they start to discolour.

Drying
Craspedia dries easily and quickly, and could even be used direct in an arrangement and left to dry in situ.

Dipsacus fullonum
TEASEL

Background
Frequenting hedgerows, road verges and waste ground, the teasel is a native to Europe. In the past, infusions or ointments were made from the roots for medical purposes, but the teasel's main value has always been in textile-making – the hooked spines of the flower-head having exactly the right degree of flexibility, and strength to tease up the nap of woollen cloth. The Fullers' teasel is a form of the common teasel, selected for its better spines.

Uses in arranging
The familiar brown teasel, which lasts outside throughout winter, has been for many years a familiar element in autumnal flower displays. It can be sprayed gold or white for Christmas use. However it can also be picked in flower and dried green.

Cultivation
The teasel is a hardy biennial and seeds freely in the wild. It flowers in its second year on tall, branched stems reaching up to 3m (9ft) high. All parts of the plant are very prickly and need thick gloves for handling.

Harvesting
As the teasel head develops, the spines are initially soft and bend to the touch. They become more firm as mauve flower buds appear between the spines. Flowering progresses in a ring up the head and as it nears completion, the greenness of the head begins to dull in colour. Pick when the ring of colour is about halfway up the head.

Drying
Drying is quick and easy as the teasel has a hollow stem but to retain colour it must be dried and stored in the dark.

Eryngium sp.
SEA HOLLY

Background
The *Eryngium* family includes a range of tough, spiny plants, from the native sea holly *E. maritimum* of coastal areas of Europe to the *E. alpinum* of the Alps. Eryngium root was once considered to be of medicinal value.

Uses in arranging
The larger forms of *Eryngium* are dramatic enough to use on their own and the smaller ones can be incorporated in posies. Though picked when at its bluest, the *Eryngium planum* does fade over time. It can, however, be dyed either green or an inky blue without looking too unnatural. *Eryngium* looks appropriate with a maritime theme, combined with shells and driftwood, but is also striking in winter displays, especially with silver spray adding a frosted look to the cool blue-grey tones.

Cultivation
There are a number of varieties which are useful both as garden plants and for floral decoration: the large-flowered, silvery biennial *E.*
giganteum, the pretty *E. bourgatti,* and the perennial blue *E. planum,* which is most commonly grown for fresh and dried flower use. The latter is hardy and trouble-free to grow in well-drained soils, and produces neat flowers on tall, branched stems about 1m (3ft) high. It is loved by bees. Propagation can be by root cuttings or it can be left to self-seed.

Harvesting
As the stem of *E. planum* grows there is a steely blue colour that spreads up and out along the branches to the flower-heads. The terminal head, which forms at a lower point than the lateral branches, is the first to come into flower and turn from pale green to blue. However, it is important to wait until the tallest flowers have turned colour and to cut when these are at their bluest. Gloves are not always necessary for picking but are advisable for handling large quantities of sea holly when dry. With some larger forms such as *E.* 'Miss Willmott's Ghost' it is the silvery grey colour which is important and the picking stage can be quite late.

Drying
Eryngium dries quickly and easily and can be used direct in displays, though colour retention may not be as good.

Eryngium 'Miss Willmott's Ghost'.

Gypsophila paniculata.

Gypsophila paniculata
BABY'S BREATH

Background
This plant grows best in chalky soils. Originating in Mediterranean regions and Eastern Europe to central Asia, it is now universally grown for commercial floristry though, surprisingly, is less frequent as a garden plant.

Uses in arranging
The frothy white form of *Gypsophila* is popular in wedding bouquets and as a delicate complement to roses and peonies. Its sturdy stems make it easy to use either full length or in short sprays.

Cultivation
Gypsophila is a deciduous perennial growing reliably on well-drained, chalky soils. The small flowers will shrink during drying so it is essential to cultivate the varieties with the largest, whitest, double-flowered heads.
   The garden flowers are rarely as large as the commercially produced, glasshouse-grown types. Nevertheless, shop-bought *Gypsophila* dries very successfully. Outdoor plants grow to about 1m (3ft), producing a mass of flowers in mid-summer, and providing continuous attraction to bees.

Harvesting
Select the whitest flowers, when they are fully open and before they start to brown. The double flowers always appear whiter than the semi-double or single flowers which, after drying, tend to look greyish.

Drying
The flowers dry very quickly hanging upside down, but the thicker stems can take a surprisingly long time to dry fully. Test dryness by snapping them at the junctions with the lateral branches. The dried bunches can be usefully dyed with soft, pastel colours.

(left to right) Carthamus tinctorius, Craspedia globosa, Dipsacus fullonum, Lonas inodora, Gypsophila paniculata.

Limonium sinuatum
STATICE

Background
Statice is native to Europe, Mediterranean regions and Asia. *Limonium* refers to the plant's native habitat of salt marshes, and the word sinuatum describes the wavy-edged leaves of this particular variety. (It was originally classified as *Statice sinuata* – the name *Statice* alluding to the plant's supposed ability to stay the flow of blood.)

Uses in arranging
For many years statice has been a cottage garden favourite, grown especially for drying. Because it dried easily it was picked, put straight into a vase, and left to dry. The stems faded, the petals accumulated dust and then a year (or several years) later it was replaced by a fresh bunch. Because it was so familiar in the past, its popularity as a dried flower has waned in recent years especially with such a wealth of exciting alternatives available. However, its versatility will ensure its continued use by those who understand its attributes.

Statice is available in a range of long-lasting colours – white, yellow, apricot, pink, lilac, blue and purple. This makes it excellent for linking with particular colour schemes, especially lilac, blue and peach – shades which few other dried flowers can provide. The apricot colour and the pure white are ideal for wedding bouquets. The dark purple is useful in hand-tied bouquets especially in dramatic contrast to oranges and yellows. The positioning of the flowers on the upper side of an arching stem allow it to be used either to form dense masses of colour or as lines to direct the eye in a display. Never a focal flower itself, it can nevertheless enhance other focal varieties.

Cultivation
Statice is a half-hardy annual, preferring full sun and tolerant of a dry soil and alkaline conditions. It needs warmth to germinate and will flower about twelve weeks later. Removal of the first flower stem will increase later productivity. The yellow statice can be used as a fresh flower, but is rarely dried commercially because of its fragility. The pink and apricot colours also need careful handling but the blue and white are relatively sturdy.

Harvesting
Statice flowers in full summer and seems to need a couple of weeks of hot sunshine for the flowers to develop fully and evenly – and they can be ruined by an ill-timed rainstorm which will severely dull the pink and apricot colours. For picking, the papery flowers must be wide open and individual stems selected as they mature. The white must not be allowed to over-mature as the centre turns brown.

Drying
Even though the statice dries happily in a vase, the fresh colour of the stems will be lost using this method. It is best dried upside down in the dark, tied in loose bunches. The winged stems are woody and dry quickly. High temperatures are not recommended as over-drying makes the flowers fragile and easily dislodged during handling. Test dryness by snapping the thickest stems.

Limonium dumosum
SEA LAVENDER OR 'DUMOSA'

Background
Limonium latifolium is the true sea lavender, native to salt marshes in Europe, and is similar to *L. carolinianum* which is found on North American coastlines. Like a finer form of *Gypsophila*, it is available as a fresh-cut item but is rarely used for drying because of its strange smell. However 'Dumosa' – a more bushy form with whiter flowers is the most widely grown for dried flower use.

Uses in arranging
As with statice, sea lavender is a species that has been somewhat over-used in the past but this is perhaps a compliment to its versatility. At one time 'Dumosa' was invariably seen as a cushion-like mound into which other flowers (especially stiff-wired *Helichrysum*) were inserted. It is much more attractive if used as a filler to finish off a display, or as a basis for swags and garlands. It takes up dye easily and so is ideal for providing soft background colours like peach, lavender blue or sea-green.

Cultivation
Being a reliable, trouble-free, perennial of neat low-growing form, it is surprising that 'Dumosa' is not more readily grown as a plant for herbaceous borders. It can be established from seed, and from a rosette of leaves it produces, in its second year, a small bush of stems about 30–45cm (12–18in) high.

Harvesting
In mid-summer, the arched, branching stems produce small, star-like, white flowers which open progressively along the stem. It is important to wait until the flowers are fully open but to pick before either the stems or the centre of the flowers start to turn brown.
It may be that some plants will flower slightly later than others, but generally all the stems on one plant will mature at the same time, making picking easy. The branched stems grow inter-meshed and some vigorous plants may produce a bunch that is too large. Gradually tease the stems apart while they are still supple and divide into smaller bunches ready for drying.

Drying
Dry in the dark to retain the greenness of the stems but dry slowly without artificial heat. This is important and in contrast to most other species. High temperatures cause the stems to arch and become brittle whereas slow drying maintains a suppleness and springiness which is more preferable to handle when arranging. 'Dumosa' can be slow-dried over several weeks, just with gentle air movement.

Lonas inodora
AFRICAN DAISY

Background
Originating in Mediterranean regions and North Africa, *Lonas* is an annual with a flower like a small garden yarrow in colour.

Uses in arranging
The stems and heads are both strongly formed, so it can be used individually in small arrangements or bouquets where golden yarrow would be too large. The colour combines well with orange *Carthamus* and *Helichrysum* or with blue larkspur.

Cultivation
Lonas is an annual which can be sown in open ground and flowers in mid-summer. It is a neat trouble-free plant which grows to 60cm (24in) high, thriving in full sun and a well-drained soil.

Harvesting
As with *Achillea*, it takes a long time for the flower to open fully and be ready for picking. It should be cropped when at its most yellow, when the stamens are visible. In the garden it can be cropped selectively but commercially it is cut in a block.

Drying
Lonas dries quickly and easily, hanging upside down.

Xeranthemum annuum
IMMORTELLE

The Greek name *xeros* 'dry' and *anthos* 'flower' describes this pretty but long-lasting annual which originates from southern Europe. It grows easily from seed and likes full sun but not too dry a soil for full productivity. It forms a neat grey mound which in summer is a mass of flowers in either white or pink. It can either be cut in a block, to give an informal mixture of buds, young and fully open flowers or it can be selectively harvested taking individual stems as they come ready. The flowers do not open further during drying. The early to full flowering stage is the most attractive; mature flowers may discolour during drying, the petals turning grey.

Xeranthemum annuum.

There are just a few species that fall into this category, which generally applies to flower bracts that remain intact late into the season. The two most familiar of these are hops and hydrangeas.

Humulus lupulus
HOPS

Background

The hop is native to Europe and botanically related to the stinging nettle. The common name comes from the Anglo-Saxon word *hoppan* meaning 'to climb'. For centuries, hops have been used as a flavouring and preservative for beer; in Victorian England the hop industry flourished as beer was part of the wages of labourers working on the construction of the early canals and railways.

The commercial production of hops for beer worldwide is limited to certain geographical bands of latitude of appropriate day-length. The majority are grown in the northern hemisphere in North America and Europe, but there are some in South Africa, New Zealand and Tasmania. Hops will grow outside these areas, but will not yield as productively.

Hops are associated with cures for insomnia – hence hop pillows and hop tea – and lupulin, a hop extract, is used in homoeopathic remedies. Its bitter taste is also sometimes used as a food flavouring.

Uses in arranging

In hop growing areas the long 'bines' of hop flowers have traditionally been used for decorating the inside of pubs and old farmhouses. In recent years the fashion for them has spread to the home and they are enthusiastically acquired for decoration as swags or garlands where they are unsurpassed for achieving instant effect. Hops are superb for festive occasions, when twined up marquee poles or church pillars, or draped over doorways and along the front of wedding tables. Small sprays of hops can be included in table centre decorations and individual hop flowers added to pot-pourri mixes.

Cultivation

Hops are dioeceous – having separate male and female plants. For the showy hop flowers, it is the female plant that is required. They grow easily from seed, though are normally purchased commercially as setts, and reach maturity in their third year. A herbaceous perennial, requiring a deep, rich, moist soil, the hop can grow at a staggering rate, as much as 60cm (24in) a week, twining clockwise up strings in commercial hop gardens or trailing through pergolas, trelliswork and trees. In warm climates stems can reach a height of 8m (24ft) during the growing season. The true flowers, which are insignificant burrs, are produced on the lateral shoots and later develop papery green 'petals' to form the familiar seed-heads which are harvested in early autumn.

Being susceptible to a soil-borne fungus known as Verticillium Wilt, which can devastate commercial crops, the beer-making varieties can usually only be purchased from licensed growers. An ornamental golden-leafed form, *H. lupulus* 'Aurea', is sometimes available from plant nurseries but is less prolific. During the growing season, hops can attract a range of pests and diseases – red spider mite, aphid, mildew – which may cause browning or yellowing of the leaves if not treated. In the autumn, the plant dies back and should be cut down to ground level and the cuttings removed to help reduce disease being carried over to the next season.

Harvesting

Hop bines are harvested in early autumn when the flower cones are a bright, fresh green, fully developed and firm to the touch. Commercially grown hop bines are usually sold as 3m (9ft) lengths of which the top end, nearer the light, is usually bushier than the base. It is a good idea to wear long sleeves when handling fresh hops as the tiny barbs on the stems can scratch delicate skin.

Drying

Hops are best hung immediately in their final decorative position and allowed to dry in situ. While the stems are fresh they can be twined freely and will drape in a natural way. They should be put in a location where they will not be accidentally knocked or blown by strong draughts since, once dry, the flower cones and leaves become brittle and can be damaged if disturbed. Hops have a distinctive aroma which is present while they are drying but soon fades unless the flower cones are crushed.

If the hop bines need to be kept for later use, they should be dried hanging up so that they are not crushed or tangled and the air can move freely between them. The thick stems take some while to dry fully. Drying in darkness is essential for colour retention. Fully dry bines will shed cones and petals like confetti when being handled but the damage can be minimized by placing them in a damp location for a few hours or overnight to take in atmospheric moisture before trying to work with them. This softens the leaves and flowers and reduces, though does not eliminate, shattering. A fine mist spray is also effective.

The tiny yellow lupulin glands on the hops (which look like pollen grains) contain sticky aromatic hop oils. These can stain hands, clothes and furnishings, so be sure to take sensible precautions, such as using dust-sheets, before putting up decorative hop bines, whether fresh or dried, in the home.

Humulus lupulus. Thick bines of commercially grown hops.

Hydrangea macrophylla *gradually changing from its summer to autumn colour.*

Hydrangea macrophylla
MOP-HEAD HYDRANGEA

Background
Forms of hydrangea have been found in China and Japan as well as North and South America. The name means water vessel.

Uses in arranging
The subtle blues, pale greens and dark reds of these glorious flowers are unbeatable for creating a massed effect of classical elegance as well as being excellent fillers in big displays. Alternatively, the heads can be divided up into clusters for inclusion in smaller arrangements.

Cultivation
These bushy deciduous shrubs can tolerate a range of soil types but the same variety that produces a blue flower on acid soil will produce a pink flower on alkaline soil. Flowers in the shade tend to be greener. A range of varieties with different growth forms and subtly different hues are available. The best for drying are the sterile mop-head 'Hortensia' types whose flowers can sometimes measure 30cm (12in) across.

(top to bottom) Eucalyptus cinerea 'Silver Dollar', Hydrangea macrophylla, Salvia officinalis.

The cream *H. paniculata* is also useful. They all prefer a good moist soil, with partial shade and shelter from frost. In hot summers it is essential to prevent the plants from drying out; once the flowers have wilted, even if only for a short time, they will never recover their quality.

Harvesting
It is not possible to preserve the bright fresh colours of the summer blooms as these young petals shrivel. A hydrangea flower must be picked as late in the season as possible. By this time it will have changed to its autumnal colouring and should feel papery, having dried out naturally. Sometimes late flowers may not have quite reached this stage before the weather dictates that they must be picked (frost can ruin flowers overnight, turning them brown). In this instance cut them, stand them in a vase with a little water and leave them to dry out slowly indoors.

Drying
Dry gently, hanging individually or in loose bunches. Fast drying has no benefit and may cause shrivelling if the heads are slightly immature.

drying leaves

Many leaves, especially those of deciduous trees, do not air-dry successfully because they either shrivel or are too easily detached from the stem. However, there are some exotic or evergreen leaves that are easy to work with such as palm fronds and leathery magnolia or laurel leaves. Large artichoke or cardoon leaves cut late in the season can be dried flat to good effect. It is always worth experimenting with drying evergreen shrubs from the garden if they are needed as filler material for arrangements in the home. Do not forget that the simple leaves of maize or sorghum can be plaited or formed into bows. Pressed ferns are also attractive.

The use of glycerine has always been popular with flower arrangers and commercial foliage producers. Oak and beech leaves are especially useful if dyeing is combined with the process to produce dark green, rich brown or burgundy foliage.

Eucalyptus sp.
GUM TREE

Background
Fast-growing eucalyptus trees provide some of the most versatile foliage for floristry work as well as oils of high medicinal value. The species originates from Australia and New Zealand and most varieties are frost tender. One of the hardiest is *E. gunnii,* a popular garden tree in temperate climates.

Uses in arranging
It is usually the juvenile foliage of eucalyptus that is cropped for floristry work. The main factor which affects the choice of varieties for drying is how firmly the leaves hold the stem. Some leaf stalks detach too readily whereas with other varieties, such as *E. gunnii* and the large grey *E. perriniana,* the leaves encircle the stem and therefore cannot break off. The leaves of *E. cinerea* 'Silver Dollar' are equally sturdy, being directly attached to the stem. Excellent as an unfading background foliage with pinks, blues and purples, it can be used in large displays or cut down into shorter lengths, making it very economical for use in table centres or compact vases.

The fine-leafed *E. parvifolia* is useful in wedding bouquets, though it needs careful handling when dry. The dark green privet-like leaf of *E. stellulata* is a strong colour but drops readily so is best used in topiary or collage work.

Cultivation
Before planting, consult the cultural details for each variety.

Harvesting
Do not cut new young foliage for drying as it will shrivel. Cut in the late autumn when the leaves have become firm and the stems have hardened.

Drying
Eucalyptus can be used fresh in arrangements and left to dry in situ, pervading the room with its powerful aroma. If being hung up in bunches it should be allowed to dry slowly; high temperatures affect the oil inside the leaves and cause a dulling of the colour. The grey eucalyptus varieties can be stored for a long time without deterioration and the long-lasting scent is a deterrent to insect pests.

Florists have always preserved eucalyptus in glycerine to give pliable leaves and stems that are easy to work with. Since this alters the colour it is best used with the dark green rather than the lighter silvery grey varieties.

The juvenile foliage of Eucalyptus gunni.

Salvia officinalis
COMMON SAGE

Background
The aromatic sage, so popular as a culinary herb, is valuable not only as a flavouring but also as an antiseptic, hence its use as a stuffing in poultry. The essential oils of sage are currently thought to contain properties that promote healing. Certainly, it was highly valued by the Chinese who would trade their tea for sage from Europe.

Uses in arranging
Bunches of the grey leaves look appropriate just hung to dry in the kitchen, but they can also be used in herb wreaths, hand-tied posies or as a contrasting filler at the front of large displays.

Salvia officinalis purpurascens.

Cultivation
Originating from southern Europe, sage is now widely grown as a reliable, trouble-free hardy perennial. It grows to 45–60cm (18-24in) in ordinary garden soil and prefers open sun but will tolerate light shade. Clary sage (grown commercially for use in perfumes) produces unusual flowering stems of pink or purple bracts which can be dried, but the common sage is better for leaves.

Harvesting
Remove flowering stems in the spring to promote leaf growth. Cut bunches of foliage in late summer or early autumn when the leaves have toughened and turned from grey-green to grey.

Drying
The leaves always curl when dried but this is not a problem as it is the overall texture of the bunch which is effective in arrangements, not individual leaves. Hang to dry and handle gently.

species to be harvested at seed pod stage

The advantage of having plants that can be cropped for their seed-pods is that the blooms can be enjoyed in the garden throughout their flowering period. Stems are often woody by this stage and tending to drying out naturally so there are no problems of heads drooping or appearance changing radically during the drying process. The decisions on picking are therefore concerned with criteria of colour or shape. Nevertheless, there is no room for complacency and the plants need to be watched just as closely as when they are in flower to determine when they are in their prime for drying. To be in their prime when they have already gone to seed is surely a major achievement of these plants and one that many people would like to emulate!

With some varieties, colour retention is critical. The greenness of the pods of honesty and the *Nigella* variety is crucial so the correct picking stage is a delicate balance between when the pods have been fully formed and when the colour starts to fade. Some plants develop their best colour as soon as they turn to seed but before the seeds are mature, such as *Atriplex* and linseed.

The shedding of seeds is part of the life-cycle of some plants, so if the decorative interest is in the seeds themselves, as with *Atriplex,* picking and drying has to be completed while the seeds are still firmly attached.

When it is the seed-holding vessel which is being preserved, as with poppies, it is important that the

(*left to right*) Lunaria biennis, Nigella orientalis '*Transformer*', Atriplex hortensis, Nigella damascena, Linum usitatissium.

pod or case is mature and fully developed so that it does not shrivel during drying.

A final factor in decision-making is, as always, the weather. Rain can cause discolouration or encourage mould, and wind can damage the delicate papery heads of species like Chinese lanterns and silver honesty.

The drying of seed-pods is quick and easy. Keep green plant material in the dark and ensure a continuous flow of warm air is applied.

The only problem with hanging bunches of seed-pods upside down is that seeds often fall out so be prepared to collect them. Poppies are notorious for creating a slippery carpet of tiny black seeds, which is why some people tie a paper bag around the heads during drying.

Storage of seed-heads needs to be in mouse-proof areas.

Allium sp.
LEEKS AND ORNAMENTAL ONIONS

Background

Garden leeks or onions will, if left to go to flower, produce ball-shaped seed-heads useful for their form even though they are neutral in colour. The stems can take a long time to dry and, in the house, the smell may not be welcome so it is probably best to dry these in a shed or garage. Slow drying will not affect their quality.

Ornamental varieties can produce large, dramatic showy heads. *Allium aflatunense* grows to over 1m (3ft) high. The smaller *A. christophii*, has a distinctive and spectacular starburst form. It is low growing, only 30–60cm (12-24in) high, so should be established, either by seed or bulb division, near the front of a border where it will then spread naturally. The mauve flowers appear in late spring or early summer and gradually dry off to leave the seed-heads, which can remain on the plants until late summer or early autumn.

Atriplex hortensis
ORACH

Background

Most commonly grown as a leaf vegetable, orach was known as mountain spinach in Eastern Europe where it originated. The young leaves of the red variety are an attractive addition to salads, but the flowering shoots must be continually removed to promote the tender young growth.

Uses in arranging

The tall spires of *Atriplex* are an unusual and eyecatching background element in big displays. The green form is fresh in colour (though inevitably fades quite quickly) and useful in combination with other natural rustic forms. The red form *Atriplex hortensis* 'Rubra' is more dramatic, being a burgundy colour, and is excellent in pink colour schemes. Careful handling is needed to prevent the seeds from shedding.

Cultivation

Sow in the spring in open ground or at the back of a herbaceous border. On a rich, well-watered soil *Atriplex* can easily grow to 2m (6ft) and may need staking if exposed to the wind. It is a hardy annual which self-seeds freely if left uncropped.

Harvesting

The round, flat seeds develop in late summer. Patience and close observation is needed and timing is critical for picking. The seeds develop in size and gradually change colour – either to a bright green or a crimson, depending on the variety. Suddenly they seem to acquire an extra intensity of colour and should be picked exactly at this stage which is just before they start to lose colour and drop. The main stems and the laterals are equally valuable and need to be cropped selectively every two days. Do not pick the stems too early as the colour will be drab and the seeds will shrivel when dried.

Allium christophii.

Drying

Dry quickly in the dark to hold colour and prevent the seeds from maturing further. Handle dried bunches gently.

Linum usitatissium
LINSEED OR FLAX

Background

Linseed has been cultivated for centuries as an agricultural crop. Its fibrous stems are the source of flax from which linen cloth is made and the seeds of linseed yield oil which is used as cattle feed or as a varnish. Medicinally it has been used to make poultices and cough remedies. Flax cloth is referred to in biblical and Greek stories and has been found in old Egyptian tombs.

Uses in arranging

If picked and dried correctly, the clusters of small, bright golden seed-pods are an eyecatching addition to floral displays. The stems are tough and require sharp scissors or secateurs to cut. Linseed combines well with grasses and orange *Carthamus* and also adds a sparkle to Christmas arrangements.

Cultivation

Linseed is an annual and usually sown in the spring but there are now some hardy varieties for autumn sowing. Its flowering period is early and brief, with delightful light blue flowers that individually only last a day. The seed-pods rapidly develop and the plant then gradually loses colour until the pods are brown – the stage at which it is harvested for oil. In the garden it is best grown in a small block that is not part of a border. Linseed will tolerate a range of soil conditions and grow to about 60cm (24in) high.

Harvesting

The time to harvest is in late spring or early summer, as soon as the seed-pods have developed and are starting to turn from green to yellow. The stem and leaves should still be green.

Drying

Unlike other varieties cut for their seed-pods, linseed is positively damaged by drying too fast. High temperatures cause the oil to discolour the heads, turning them brown. The trick is to dry them in the dark, to preserve the green, just with gentle warmth. The fibrous stems dry quickly but the seed-pods take a long time and it may be two or three weeks before the bunches are dry enough to store safely without the risk of mould developing. Test dryness by crushing a pod and trying to break the brown seeds in half with a fingernail – they crack when dry.

Lunaria biennis
HONESTY

Background

The Latin name describes the flat, round, silvery, moon-like seed pods. As an annual, *Lunaria* is native to southern Europe but the biennial form is now found throughout Europe and North America.

Uses in arranging

Traditionally, honesty has been grown for its autumnal seed-pods the delicate papery white circles often being combined with bright orange Chinese lanterns for winter displays. To achieve this effect, however, the dull outer skins of the pod need to be gently peeled off and the seeds removed to reveal the shimmering inner skin. Such a labour-intensive exercise is

not commercially viable and so honesty has always tended to be grown in the garden and gathered for sale at autumn craft fairs rather than being available through florists.

Current fast-drying techniques have created the option of drying honesty while the pods are still green and using it as a fresh-coloured filler instead of *Carthamus* or grasses. It can also be dyed burgundy or terracotta to give it greater versatility.

Cultivation

Honesty grows well in sun or partial shade and tolerates poor soils. It germinates easily and will flower in the spring of the following year. White- or mauve-flowered varieties are available and this does marginally influence the shade of the seed-pod – either bright green or tinged burgundy. The plant grows to about 1m (3ft), with stiff, branched stems. It is suscep-tible to club root.

Harvesting

At the green stage, honesty is ready to harvest in late spring. At first the seed-pods are very soft and bendy, but gradually become more firm to the touch. Pick as soon as the topmost pods have reached this stage, before the lower ones start to lose colour.

If picking in the autumn, wait as long as possible until the stem has dried out but before the delicate papery moons have been torn by the wind.

Drying

The later-picked stems need no additional drying. The green pods must be dried in the dark.

Nigella damascena
LOVE-IN-A-MIST

Background

Niger, meaning black, refers to the small black seeds held within the round, green and red-striped seed-pod which is itself surrounded by a 'mist' of finely-cut delicate leaves. The plant originates from Mediterranean regions but since the 16th century has been widely grown as a delightful and reliable cottage garden plant. In the past the seeds were sometimes used as a substitute for pepper and it was thought that if crushed and mixed with vinegar they could remove freckles!

Uses in arranging

The colour and shape are extremely useful with other flowers, such as in a simple combination with red roses and *Gypsophila*. Arranged in clusters, it is a useful filler (as a green alternative to grasses, and more delicate than *Carthamus*), or the heads can be individually placed in small dense, dome-shaped posies.

Cultivation

Sow direct in the autumn or spring but do not transplant. Love-in-a-mist is a hardy annual and, once established, will seed freely and return year after year. Available with white, pink, and light or dark blue flowers, the best variety for drying is the dark blue 'Miss Jekyll' – this has the most pronounced purple striations on the seed pods. The flowers, which appear in early summer, are a delightful addition to a garden.

(left to right) Papaver somniferum *'Hen and Chickens'*, Papaver somniferum, Papaver dubium.

Harvesting

After flowering, the pods take about three to four weeks to develop, growing in size, deepening in colour and becoming firm to the touch. Do not pick them too soon or they will shrivel and be hidden by the feathery leaf fronds. Leave them as long as possible but pick before they start to discolour.

Drying

Dry in the dark, hanging upside down. Bunches dry very quickly and seeds can be collected for sowing.

Nigella orientalis 'Transformer'
TRANSFORMER

This variety has yellow flowers similar in form to *N. damascena* but the seed-pod is strikingly different – it develops into a bright green crown. Its shape and texture are very effective in topiary trees or Christmas decorations. It is best sown in the spring but germination may be erratic. Harvest when the seed-head has become firm and cannot be squashed between a thumb and finger, but before it starts to discolour.

Nigella orientalis *'Transformer' seed heads beginning to develop.*

Papaver somniferum.

Papaver somniferum
OPIUM POPPY

Background
Poppies range from the common red poppy, *Papaver rhoes* and *P. dubium* with its small elongated pods, to the large and showy perennial oriental poppy. The common poppy is an invasive annual in arable fields and waste ground in many temperate areas. But the type most widely grown is the opium poppy which originated in Asia but was known by the Ancient Greeks and Romans. The word *somniferum* describes its power as a sedative or somnolent. The latin word *pap* and the greek word *opos* mean 'sap or juice' and it is the sap in the stem and seed-head which has the narcotic power.

The opium poppy is legally grown for the manufacture of morphine and codeine. Its seeds (which are not narcotic) are used in food decoration and can be crushed to produce oil. In hot climates, such as parts of Asia and South America, the poppy produces a very potent sap which is used for the illegal production of heroin.

Uses in arranging
The poppy is exceptionally versatile and a constant favourite with arrangers. Its attributes are sturdiness, bold form and a neutral colour. It does not take up dye easily but can be coated in a range of surface paint colours including gold, which is ideal for festive decorations.

Cultivation
Cultivation is restricted in some countries unless licensed. *Papaver somniferum* is a hardy annual. For drying, select a variety with large pods. Sown in the spring, it will grow to 75cm (30in) and flower in mid-summer with papery, short-lived white petals with a crimson blotch at the base. It is trouble-free to establish and grow, the only danger to the the seed-heads being rain at harvest time which can cause a dark speckling.

Harvesting
As the seed-pod matures, it changes from green to a blue-grey, develops a surface bloom and gradually hardens further and turns a biscuit-grey colour. If picked green it will shrivel, if picked at the grey stage it may shrink slightly, but if picked when biscuit-coloured it will hold its shape well. For another indication of maturity, cut open a seed-head. Immature heads contain white seeds, but seeds that are beginning to darken indicate that cropping can begin. The stem can bend or snap easily so handle with care.

Drying
There is little moisture remaining in the plant at this stage and no green colour to be preserved so drying is quick and easy and need not be in the dark. The seeds turn black quickly and will pour out of the upturned head so be ready to catch them.

Papaver somniferum
'HEN AND CHICKENS'

This extraordinary variety is similar in growth to the opium poppy but with crimson petals, and the seed-head has a frill of tiny pods around the base. The appearance is of a hen sitting on a nest or surrounded by little chicks. Being so unusual, it always draws comment and is often best displayed on its own in a simple vase. It is particularly susceptible to damage from rain, with water collecting around the base of the pod and allowing mould to develop.

Physalis franchetii
CHINESE LANTERN OR CAPE GOOSEBERRY

Physalis has always been grown, both in Europe and the Far East, both for its decorative bright orange lanterns and for the berries which, in some varieties, are edible. A herbaceous perennial, it can be grown from seed or, more reliably, from root cuttings. It will tolerate full sun but prefers light shade with a deep rich soil. It should be cut as late as possible in the autumn but before the leaves discolour or the lanterns are damaged and skeletonized by wind and rain.

The stems can be used fresh in displays or garlands or left to dry in the dark to retain leaf and stem colour. It is one of the few varieties that must be dried upright. If hung upside down, the lanterns bend over the wrong way and are then liable to snap when the stems are turned up the right way. There is no advantage to fast drying since it takes a long time for the little tomato-like fruit to shrivel. Do not pack for storage until the fruit are completely dry.

Physalis franchetii.

drying grasses

Phalaris canariensis showing the development of the head from early flower until it starts to lose colour. The middle stage is the ideal time to cut for drying.

There is a vast array of grass varieties that can be dried successfully, from the shimmering little quaking grass to the familiar cereal crops like wheat or the giant ornamental pampas grass. They can offer strong forms, delicate textures, fresh greenness, height, direction or rustic charm to a display. For some varieties, such as bulrushes, there is only one possible picking stage. For others, there is a choice of cutting when they are in flower for the best green colour, or at the traditional harvest stage when they have developed seed. Beware: the pollen abundant on grasses cut in flower may cause problems with hay-fever or skin allergies.

When testing for dryness in grasses, check the stems in the centre of the bunch, underneath the rubber band. The stems should snap easily.

Grasses bearing seeds will obviously be a temptation to mice, so store in sealed boxes in rodent-free areas. Putting mothballs in the boxes is also a deterrent.

CEREAL CROPS

Avena, Hordeum, Triticum, and Triticale
OATS, BARLEY, WHEAT AND BEARDED WHEAT

Background
These staple crops, grown throughout temperate regions, are cheap and readily available to purchase and therefore popular in displays. In many areas it was a tradition to keep a sheaf of wheat in the home from one harvest until the next as a charm to ensure the success of the next crop.

Uses in arranging
In the past, grasses featured as the pale golden stems in autumnal arrangements along with poppies, teasels and honesty. Now that they are available in a choice of colours from natural green and gold to dyed, they are in demand throughout the year. Natural green oats provide excellent filler material for mixed displays, while golden oats are particularly striking with greys, blues and pale yellows.

Barley, grown mainly as a cattle feed or for malting, has long thin awns which have a distinctly rustic charm. The green head is usually too thin for visual impact. The golden stage is better for drying but the awns that terminate the seed are easily broken so need careful handling.

Wheat is the most important of the cereals and was often used as a symbol of fertility, especially at country weddings. It is especially popular in the autumn, either in its green or golden state, for the making of stooks or sheaves for harvest festivals and Thanksgiving celebrations. Because of its strong sculptural form, it can be stylishly used on its own.

Bearded wheat (the type used for the making of pasta) is a cross between wheat and

Triticale being commercially cut and bunched by machine.

rye. It also has awns like barley but these are shorter and sturdier. They give the head a fullness which is especially useful in the making of free-standing stooks. *Triticale* is best cut at the flowering stage, when it is a soft blue-green colour.

Harvesting
Cropping must be either at flowering or at golden seed stage and emphatically not anytime in between or the colour will look pale and washed-out. Because fast drying is essential, cut only in dry weather after the dew has gone. The bunches shrink significantly during drying so ensure they are well secured with rubber bands.

The best time for cropping green grasses in their prime lasts about four to five days. After the topmost 'flag' leaf has been formed, the young green head emerges and immediately starts to flower. Wait to pick until the top of the head has developed beyond the tip of the flag leaf; by this time the head will have filled out in size and the resultant bunch will not look too leafy. As soon as flowering is complete, the head starts to pale in colour. Put bunches in the dark as soon as they are cut to prevent sunlight reacting adversely with the green chlorophyll.

Harvesting at the golden stage should be done a little before the crops would normally be cropped for seed in order to obtain the best colour (bad weather and natural ageing can cause discoloration) and to minimize seed loss. If cut at the normal harvest time for grain the heads tend to disintegrate more easily when dried. Barley ears bend over as they ripen which can make them more difficult to bunch, hang, and store in quantity so, unless that aspect of its character is particularly required, it is a good idea to cut it while it is still upright, before it has 'necked' over.

Drying
Green grasses need fast drying to maintain colour – and even then there can be a noticeable difference between the colour of the green outer and yellow inner leaves of a bunch. If drying grasses at home, keep bunches small and hang them upside down with room between for air to circulate. Leaves can be stripped before drying if wished. Test dryness at the centre of a bunch, under the band, by snapping the stems.

Golden crops dry quickly and easily since they are already half-dry when cut.

(clockwise from left) Zea mais, Phalaris canariensis, Briza mazima, Typha latifolia, Typha minima, Triticum, Triticale, Lagurus ovatus, Bromus macrostachys.

ORNAMENTAL GRASSES

Bromus macrostachys, Briza mazima, Lagurus ovatus, Phalaris canariensis
BROME, QUAKING GRASS, HARE'S TAIL, CANARY GRASS

Background
These are just a few of the many grasses that can be dried to provide a range of textures and shapes, but the general rules can be applied to other ornamental grasses in the garden.

Uses in arranging
Brome, a perennial, has a full head and is ideal as a filler but is not as big or rustic in character as oats. The delicate quaking grass is more important for its quaintness of form than its colour and is very pretty in little posies with flowers such as marjoram and *Alchemilla*. The fluffy hare's tail is a hardy annual of a naturally pale creamy colour and takes up dye easily. This attribute has tended to be exploited commercially, sometimes making it a vehicle for gaudy and unnatural colourings.

Canary grass, also a hardy annual which can be sown in the autumn, has a neat spear-shaped head ideal for use in compact or sculptured arrangements. It can also be dyed well and is useful as a filler when dyed terracotta, burgundy or blue shades.

Cultivation
Follow the cultivation instructions for the individual varieties.

(left to right) Avena sativa, Sorghum nigra, Setaria viridis, Zea mais, Panicum miliaceum, Setaria italica, Hordeum.

Harvesting
The canary and brome grasses are best harvested when in flower and as fresh a colour as possible. The ears have usually extended well beyond the top leaf by this time, but will rapidly begin to bleach in colour if left longer. The hare's tail and quaking grass are more dependent on texture than colour and can be picked a little later when the heads have developed in size. The quaking grass hangs better when it has more weight in the heads but will disintegrate if left to mature fully.

Drying
All these varieties have thin stems and dry quickly. Never-theless, the rules of fast drying in the dark, still apply to maintain quality. The heads of *Lagurus* are particularly tempting to mice as soft bedding material, so store with care.

Panicum miliaceum, P. violaceum, Setaria italica, S. viridis, Sorghum nigra
MILLETS AND SORGHUM

Background
Millet and sorghum are annual grasses grown as agricultural crops for their seed in hot climates. Apart from their food value for human consumption, millets are also sold widely in pet shops. The large golden heads of Italian millet are familiar adornments of budgerigar cages, and the small round seeds of panicum millet are a major constituent of bird-seed.

Uses in arranging
Whereas wheat and other winter-sown cereal crops take about two months for the seeds to mature after flowering, these grasses take only a few weeks. The advan-tage of this to the florist is that the plant has not had time to senesce and lose its freshness and so presents a good green colour combined with the fullness of a seed-head. In the case of the panicum millet – *Panicum miliaceum* – the weight of the seed gives the head a softness and movement as it gently trails, making it ideal for pedestal displays or hanging baskets. There is also a darker form, *Panicum violaceum,* which has a looser structure to the head.

Italian or foxtail millet – *Setaria italica* – has a blunt, fat green head which is useful in 'country garden' arrangements along with larkspur and peonies. It is sturdy but retains a softness of shape. The more delicate *Setaria viridis* is suited to displays of a smaller scale – even as small as buttonholes!

The large lance-shaped head of sorghum is a very bold form, excellent for the background of large displays. It can be cut when the head is still green and the seeds small and tightly packed or later when it has turned a rich brown.

The latter stage is useful as the colour holds well. The long leaves of sorghum are strong and can be included in arrangements or made into bows or plaited ties.

Cultivation
Sorghum and millet need warm soil temperatures for germination. When grown for ornamental purposes in northern Europe and other cool temperate areas their growing season is therefore short. Sown in the mid to late spring, when ground tempera-tures have warmed, the head does not emerge until the summer. To complete its life cycle it has to rapidly flower, set seed and mature.

Harvesting
With the millets, wait until the seed-head has extended beyond the top leaf but cut before the colour starts to go. Sorghum grows strong and tall with very sturdy stems. The top leaf is long, often extend-ing beyond the head, and is not a guide to the picking stage – the stems should be cut when the seeds have reached the desired colour.

Drying
Dry fast, hanging in the dark. panicum millet tends to develop a little during the drying process, with the seeds becoming more prominent and giving a golden tinge to the head. All these varieties contain seed so must be stored away from mice.

Typha latifolia, Typha minima
REEDMACE OR BULRUSHES

These bulrushes look wonderful on their own in tall vases but unless properly dried there can be disastrous results when the brown seed-heads 'explode' – which they will do easily if not cut and dried properly. If ripe, the heads can dramatically turn

Setaria italica.

themselves inside out and distribute drifts of downy white seeds. The trick is to cut the heads as soon as they turn from green to brown and dry them as quickly as possible. Even then, they need gentle handling to prevent damage. A useful tip is to apply hair spray to the dried heads to fix them more firmly. The smaller variety is obviously quicker to dry and less likely to 'blow'.

Zea mais
MAIZE

Background
Maize is grown as a staple crop throughout the world for its distinctive 'cobs' of yellow seeds which are dried and ground into flour, made into breakfast cereals and used as cattle and poultry food. The more succulent varieties (which shrivel when dried) are eaten fresh as sweetcorn.

Uses in arranging
For flower arrangers, maize offers two distinctly different forms because the flower and the seed develop separately on the same plant. The flowering stems and leaves are useful fillers for large displays, particularly those of

The flowering stems of Zea mais *ready to harvest. The maize cobs develop later in the season.*

a rustic character. The cobs are dramatic and eyecatching in bold arrangements. Miniature 'strawberry' cobs and orna-mental varieties with coloured cobs are also available.

Cultivation
Maize is an annual plant which grows up to 3m (9ft) high, producing a biscuit-coloured flowering stem in late summer. The cobs form lower down the stem and are ready to harvest in early autumn. Sow in a block and protect from strong winds. Only the varieties with tough kernels are suitable for drying; the others will shrivel.

Harvesting and drying
Cut the flowering stem when it has extended to the height of the topmost leaf or beyond and the pollen-bearing anthers are visible. The leaves are excellent for making decorative bows and can be shaped when fresh or dried. Maize 'tops' dry quickly and easily but should be kept in the dark. Test dryness by snapping the thicker stems.

Cut the cobs in the autumn when the yellow seeds have hardened enough to resist the pressure of a fingernail. The cobs are dense and are best left to dry out naturally over a long period of time. The pale leaves forming the husk can be left intact during drying and peeled back later to display the yellow cob.

exotic varieties

There are a number of plant species native to Australia and South Africa which are perennial shrubs or have a shrub-like growth. Having adapted to dry, arid conditions, they are woody and therefore hold their form when dry. Many, in fact, dry naturally on the bush. Their floral interest lies in their shapes and textures since their colourings are predominantly soft or neutral. Because they are native shrubs, the cropping of those growing in the wild is only allowed under licence.

One of the most popular and distinctive of Australian shrubs is the *Banksia* which provides florists with a range of different-sized flower-heads in soft yellow or orange colourings, each surrounded by a ruff of decorative serrated leaves. *Banksia hookeriana, B. menzii, B. occidentalis. B. prionotes, B. spectrum* and *B. speciosa* are just some of the useful varieties. The larger heads can be cut into horizontal slices to provide novel shapes for modern designs.

Sago, Lachnostachys eriobotrya, has clusters of small, off-white bobbles resembling tiny cotton-wool balls, borne on soft, furry, grey stems. It needs to be picked when still white, before it turns grey. The lower stem is woody but the flowering tip is soft. The heads often have a tendency to droop and this should be taken into account when designing a display.

Verticordia eriocephala or *V. brownii,* is also known as wild cauliflower because of its dense twiggy mounds of creamy flower heads. The branching form of the woody bunches is reminiscent of

heather and it is best displayed in a mass. Containing little moisture, it can be arranged fresh and left to dry.

The aptly named Kangaroo paw (*Anizoganthos*) with its distinctive yellow flowers is popular as a fresh-cut stem but equally useful when dried. It can be grown indoors as a conservatory plant.

A favourite is the white Australian daisy, *Ixodia,* which has a mass of neat flat-petalled flowers on the end of strudy branched stems. It is very easy to arrange and its clarity of colour is always eyecatching.

Of the South African varieties popular as cut flowers, the *Protea* is the most popular (and is frequently confused with flowering artichokes). As with the Australian *Banksia* family, they grow in a range of sizes and forms with a circle of decorative leaves surrounding the flower. They are easy to dry, and their muted colourings last well. The woody base rosettes of the *Protea* flowers are often used (natural or dyed) with other exotics. Many South African plants of shrubby structure dry well, though may lose their leaves with handling.

Though an annual rather than a shrub, and only grown in very hot climates, the cotton plant is worth a mention here. It is sometimes available through flower markets and always intrigues people who have never seen cotton in its natural state. On dry, brown stems, the balls of 'cotton wool' (*Gossypium*) are the seed-heads, containing large black seeds. Cotton is an appropriate species to adorn a bathroom or dressing room!

■ A SUMMARY

This chapter has covered some of the main varieties considered to be commercially viable for drying and others that are familiar garden plants, but the list is only a taster for the many species whose forms can be preserved. Before attempting to preserve any plant material, decide which of the plant's floral, textural, structural, tonal or aromatic qualities are required. To achieve the preservation of those qualities, look at the botanical structure of the plant, monitor its stages of development, and then select the time of harvesting and the method of drying that is appropriate. After a few experiments with some different flowers, the lessons learned can then be applied to the wide range of other plants that have not featured here. But the most important rule is to be adventurous and to enjoy the beauty that the plants have to offer.

(clockwise from central flower)
Gossypium, Anizoganthos, Sago Lachnostachys eriobotrya, Banksia *sp., sliced* Banksia *sp.,* Phylacium *sp.,* Protea *sp., sliced* Banksia *sp.,* Ixodia *sp.,* Vertricordia brownii, Banksia *sp.*

DRIED FLOWER ARRANGING

– ESSENTIAL EXTRAS

The versatility of the textures and colours provided by dried flowers has extended people's perceptions of what can be done with all types of plant material. The choice now available to flower arrangers is truly unending and the resultant experimentation with new forms, ideas and shapes is fascinating to watch. The imagination can run riot. Bizarre seed-pods, leaves and moss are being imported from all over the world, new uses are being found for old materials like driftwood or recycled metal and all sorts of other items are being incorporated, such as feathers and rope.

Containers can range from antique vases to coconut halves or old boots. Anything is possible – all that is needed is inventiveness, courage and a sense of fun. The resources are all there not only to produce highly individual arrangements but to personalize parts of the home and create long-lasting mementoes.

So, before embarking on a project, remember, there are things other than flowers to incorporate in your designs.

(opposite page) A very personalized beachcombing display using driftwood and cardoons.

flowers for free

One practical way to improvise and personalize your project to make use of items that can be found in any garden – the flowers for free. Leaves, twigs, cones, nuts and stems are all items that can be collected from the garden. Leaves can be air-dried, preserved with glycerine or pressed and used for collages or to decorate containers. Short twigs (vine is especially good) can be tied in bundles and sprayed gold as festive trimmings. Cones of all shapes and sizes can be incorporated in wreaths. Nuts can be varnished. Branches of red dogwood, corkscrew hazel or twisted willow, cut after the leaves have fallen, form distinctive displays on their own or can be decorated seasonally with painted eggs or Christmas decorations (see the alternative Christmas tree on page 138). Simple birch twigs painted white are gloriously wintry.

■ OFF-CUTS

Off-cut pieces left over from other arrangements can be bundled or re-used. Think twice before throwing away lavender and wheat stems; tied with twine, ribbon or raffia they can be used to decorate pots or wreaths. In the pot illustrated on page 23, Chinese lanterns have been glued on to wheat stems with dramatic effect. Sturdy stems of sunflowers or straight willow can be bound to form frameworks for lattice or collage designs and pliable lengths of clematis, vine or hop can be wound and intertwined to make wreath bases.

flotsam and jetsam

Beachcombing is an enjoyable activity at any age, but even more so if it has a purpose. The recent fascination for things nautical has introduced shells, pebbles, old nets, ropes and corks into floral designs. Imported sponges, loofahs, shells, dried seaweeds and starfish all offer new shapes and textures to work with but, before buying, it is advisable to check that they come from an environmentally sustainable source and that their acquisition has not damaged their natural habitat.

■ BEACHCOMBING DISPLAY

All too often the souvenirs of beachcombing, enthusiastically collected, remain forgotten in the garage for years. Creating souvenirs from these collections is a satisfying record of the holiday and an activity for all the family. The illustration opposite is such an example, made to record a walking holiday on the west coast of Scotland. The design comprises a wooden 'vase' made from driftwood – pieces of old fish boxes weathered by the sea and washed up on the beach. These were roughly nailed together (when working with driftwood, carpentry skills need only be basic). A small hole was bored into the top of the taller back-board and a hanging device made simply from wire and twig. Part of an old metal fishing float, some barnacle-covered shells, seaweed, old rope and a few seagull feathers were glued to the wood. The only part of the display not actually acquired on holiday was the bunch of cardoon flowers – but they do strongly resemble the thistle which is the emblem of Scotland.

moss, fungi and lichens

MOSS

Fresh moss is valuable to florists as a basis for wreaths, swags and hanging baskets. With the popularity of dried flowers has come a wider use of other types of moss, as well as lichen and fungi. Differentiating between these botanical categories can sometimes be confusing but, very simply, a moss is a herbaceous plant without stamens or pistils (that is, having no proper flowers), which generally prefers a damp or boggy habitat. There are two distinctive types used for dried flower work – flat moss and bun moss. (Reindeer moss is, in fact a lichen – see below.)

The bright green flat moss (sometimes preserved with dye to enhance its colour) comes in turf-like sheets. When selecting flat moss for purchase, choose pieces with a neat compact surface. It is superb used as a new covering for unsightly containers or for geometric topiary shapes. The illustration opposite shows the flat moss used to transform an ordinary plastic garden urn (on the left) into a stylish container and to create the bantam hen and cockerel. (The base shapes were formed of chicken wire on to which the pieces of flat moss were attached with a hot glue gun.) Flat moss glued to foam cones was also used for the topiary forest on page 151. Single topiary cones like this, in individual painted pots, make interesting ornaments for the mantelpiece, especially if made in matching pairs. Small pieces of moss were also tucked into the gold and white 'celebration' wall swag on page 146 to cover the foam base and to contrast with the cream flower and fabric colours.

Bun or cushion moss forms distinctive neat, dense mounds. Solid and chunky, it is useful as a ground cover in pots around the stems of topiary trees, or in collage designs. In the garden chair shown on the endpiece, it has been used to cover a hessian cushion, with the edge trimmed in Spanish moss. It can be attached either with glue or with wires which have been bent into a hairpin shape (known as 'mossing pins').

Tillandsia or Spanish moss is in fact an air plant found trailing from tree branches in hot, humid climates. Stringy in form, it is naturally grey in colour, so can be usefully dyed to other colours such as dark green. Its texture makes it a good filler material. It can be fixed with glue or wires.

FUNGI

Fungi are also non-flowering plants or moulds without chlorophyll. They feed on organic matter and are therefore found growing on other plant material. Some types, like the familiar mushrooms or toadstools, are fast growing and thus have a high water content. This means they can only be successfully dried by freeze-drying, which maintains the cell structure. However, there are some varieties that are very woody and hold their shape perfectly when dried.

The Indian sponge mushroom (used at the base of the topiary tree on page 151) is a large bracket fungus that looks good with exotic seed-heads or pieces of gnarled wood. Chestnut-coloured, chalice-shaped, shiny 'golden' mushrooms are especially versatile in combination with dried fruit and spices

and they look good with terracotta pots. They are included in the hanging basket on page 150. The South American 'calice' fungi are a rich velvety brown. They are hard when dry, but soaking in water makes them soft like chamois leather, so they can be shaped as required before being redried.

LICHENS

Lichens are similar to fungi, being non-flowering and without chlorophyll but are parasitic on algae. They are therefore to be found growing on minerals (rocks, roof tiles, stones) as well as associated with plant material such as tree bark. Lichen is generally very slow growing and is particularly sensitive to air quality; its presence is an indication of air purity.

The most widely available type of lichen is confusingly referred to as reindeer moss because it grows prolifically in Arctic regions and is grazed by the deer. Long before it became so fashionable for floristry work, its neat branching form was used to represent trees and bushes in model-making. Though naturally spongy, it goes hard when dry. If purchased dried it can be wetted to give pliability for working with, however most reindeer moss is treated to retain its softness. It is available in its natural silvery-grey, or dyed to a range of soft, bright or dark greens as well as reds, pinks and terracotta colours. The slower-growing, grey oak 'moss' (a lichen) and flat lichen (generally associated with rock) are also available. The latter is often glued on to foam to create apple or pear shapes. These species are inevitably of more dubious origin.

As with some of the maritime objects – shells, sponges, dried starfish and others – it is often difficult (if not impossible) when buying exotic fungi and lichen to establish the country of origin of these items, let alone the ecological sustainability of the methods by which they have been collected. This poses a moral dilemma especially when purchasing a product like the flat lichen which is slow growing and not the sort of species to be commercially produced and which therefore must presumably have been collected in the wild.

Continued pressure from customers for more information will hopefully put pressure on suppliers to ensure the ecological viability of their products. However, the use of what would otherwise be surplus or waste products – such as coconut shells, palm leaves or corn husks – has much to recommend it.

The moss-covered plastic urn on the left is filled with blocks of dry foam which hold bay leaves and linseed while the stone urn displays carline thistles. The topiary cockerel was made of flat moss, with a tail and ruff of panicum millet. A piece of the red flower appropriately named cockscomb (Celosia) adds fitting colour.

fruits, vegetables and spices

FRUITS

Dried apple and orange slices, whole mandarins, green lemons (which look like limes) and pomegranates are superb for their shape, character and – in the case of oranges – their scent. Strung on twine (maybe interspersed with bay leaves), or incorporated in wreaths, they are brilliant for the decoration of kitchen or eating areas and for adding to the seasonal mood at Thanksgiving and Christmas. The pomegranates can be lightly sprayed with bronze or gold for a festive look.

VEGETABLES

The craze for dried fruit has led to experiments with all sorts of vegetables. Dried slices of beetroot and carrot are somewhat limited in appeal, but bright red mini pumpkins are exceptional and so too are the big red chilli peppers – the latter being traditionally dried tied in long strings. Small round chillis can also be useful, especially in collages, but the dust from them can be unpleasant if caught in the throat. Pumpkins and chilli peppers are used in the kitchen hanging basket on page 150, along with dried fungi, artichokes, wheat and maize cobs.

SPICES

The most popular of the spices used by flower arrangers is called cinammon, though is in fact usually the lower grade cassia. It is thicker and coarser than true cinnamon and does not have such a strong scent which is why it is cheaper to buy. It is available in sizes ranging from small broken pieces for pot-pourri to sticks up to 1.5m (5ft) in length. It is often displayed tied with raffia in small bundles (see the display of Australian flowers on page 95 and the winter door ring on page 136). Cinnamon and cassia are both the bark of trees in the laurel family. The bark is rolled into 'quills' and dried. Cassia originates from northern Burma but is now widely grown in the Far East and central America. Most cinnamon is grown in Sri Lanka, from where it originates, but production has spread to India, Indonesia, Brazil and the West Indies.

Many other spices are small but invaluable for their scent. Pomanders of cloves stuck into oranges are a traditional favourite but decorations can also be made of star anise glued on to foam balls.

Sometimes leftovers from the food industry are recycled for decorative use – the centres of corn cobs can be wired on to wreaths and the outer leaves bound together to form corn husk 'dolls' or woven into wire sculptures. Fruit stones and dried orange peel can be incorporated in pot-pourri mixes. Coconut halves, still with their thick outer layer of coir, make unusual containers for candles or flowers. Coconut fibre – either natural brown or dyed green – has a tangled quality useful as a filler or for making ornamental birds' nests.

A collage of extras displayed on a framework of hazel sticks – various empty seed pods from the Amazon, mini pumpkins and round chillies, dyed coconut fibre and reindeer moss, dried beans and fungi, a piece of Palma Real, *a* Protea *and a bundle of* Assegai *sticks.*

'exotics' from around the world

Many of what are termed as 'exotics' in the floristry trade are leaves, stems or seed-pods that naturally have a tough fibrous character. These are invariably native species found in the wild and, if they are dead leaves, dried stems or empty seed cases, their collection does no ecological damage. The main threat to these species is from logging activities, especially in the Amazon jungle, where the native trees are being felled in vast areas.

THE AMERICAS

The South American range of exotics comes predominantly from the region of the Amazon basin. They are collected by native Indians in the jungle and transported by dug-out canoe to collection places along the river and from there to the coast for transport to Europe and North America. Most are brown or neutral in colour but the variety of shapes and textures is extensive – from the large smooth *Orelha de Burro* 'donkeys ear' leaves, to the round flat *Girasol Espinho* 'spiny sunflowers' and the hard cones of Uxi da Amazonia. Some seed-cases are round and massive, like the *Sapocaia*, and some are long and trumpet-shaped like *Sapocainha*. There are mock chillies (chalky white, not red) and thick, stubby palm leaves and the delicate, flower-like, pinky-brown seed-cases of *Rosa de Tefe* used in the bowls at the front of the display on page 95.

INDIA AND THE EAST

From India and the Far East come an assortment of seed-cases, sometimes mounted on false stems for ease of arrangement – bell cups, wild lily and the familiar dark brown lotus heads which are the seed-pods of a water lily – as well as bamboo and various dried palm leaves and grass stems. One of these, called 'ting ting,' is a fibrous stem that has been split into fine strips. Its straight form can be displayed alone in a stylish free-standing bundle, but it is also available with the ends twisted – known as 'curly ting ting' – and is extremely versatile. The photograph on page 90 shows it in a metal vase just finished with natural reindeer moss around the base of the stems. Florists also use just a few stems to transform a bouquet of fresh flowers, giving it flair and modernity. Split canes are available coiled into cone shapes and other stems are coiled to make 'tail springs'. Grasses are sometimes plaited or woven into baskets and dried ferns are bound into forms representing fruit or animals. The sculptural possibilities seem endless.

Strong palm leaves can be trimmed to form fan shapes and it is the large thin leaves of the raffia palm that are shredded to form the material used for many years by gardeners and flower arrangers. Apart from being a natural tie – such an ideal finishing touch to dried flowers – it is now available in a range of complementary colours.

c o n t a i n e r s

THE CHOICE

One of the major delights of working with dried
flowers is that not only do the stems not need to
be in water, but they do not need to be in
containers at all! They can be glued on to hats or
mirror frames, hung from beams, tied into sheaves,
laid in bouquets or wired on to branches.
Containers can be traditional vases, copper pots,
pottery, glass, metal buckets, wire frameworks,
wooden tubs or basketware.

The pliable stems of willow and hazel have
always been used in Europe and North America for
making baskets and other containers, but in recent
years most basketware has been imported from the
Far East using an assortment of local materials
from coconut fibre to aerial roots.

Clear glass containers are not so easy to use for
dried flowers as they are with fresh ones – mainly
because the dried flowers often need a support
system. Clever solutions are therefore needed, such
as filling the vase with pot-pourri, stones, moss or
any other interesting texture (even spare furnishing
fabric) to conceal whatever 'mechanics' of foam or
wire are at the centre.

DECORATING CONTAINERS

It is fun to disguise ordinary cheap containers, such
as jam jars or bottles. Try binding them with coils
of twine, hiding them under a 'fence' of cassia
sticks, or covering them with a layer of gold-
sprayed leaves. Vases and jugs that are cracked or
no longer a fashionable shape or design can be

*A metal vase filled with
curly ting ting creates a
versatile and long-lasting
minimalist design.*

transformed into something totally different by a
coat of reindeer moss or a tangle of coconut fibre
decorated with fruit slices. Even cheap plastic
garden urns can be transformed into elegant
classical pieces by a covering of dry moss. In the
illustration on page 107, half a dozen mini bales of
hay have been tightly tied with twine around a
very ordinary plastic flower bowl which contains
the foam supporting the bulrushes.

THEMING CONTAINERS

The choice of containers or bases is particularly
important in displays designed on a theme. Old
terracotta garden pots, watering cans and rusty
buckets are always popular for an informal, natural
look, but the imagination can stretch further – why
not use an old leather boot? Where a background
structure is required to support a wall display,
consider allowing parts of it to remain visible. Use
wicker fencing, pieces of driftwood roughly nailed
together, fishing net or slatted blinds to provide
frameworks of texture and character.

sundries for use in arrangements

Most of the florists' sundries needed to construct dried arrangements are the same as those required for fresh flowers: secateurs, wire cutters, pot tape, 'frogs' for securing foam on to a base, reel wires for binding, self-sealing tape for concealing stems, setting clay for weighting containers, plaster of Paris for fixing topiary trunks, chicken-wire, candle holders and, of course, stub wires.

WIRING

The thicker wires (particularly 90-gauge or 0.9mm) tend to be used more than thinner or rose wires. Wiring is a crucial technique to master with dried flowers. It is important for four reasons: first, because the flowers shrink when dried, more of them are needed to create an effect and sometimes there is not space in the foam base to take this quantity, especially if they are thick. Groups of stems may therefore need to be wired together so that only the wire needs to be inserted in the base.

Secondly, smaller flower-heads – such as lavender, cornflower or *Anaphalis* – need to be grouped in tight clusters to have visual impact.

Thirdly, the stems of fleshy varieties such as *Helichrysum* are fragile when dried. They cannot easily be inserted into the foam without breaking and need to be wired to provide support.

Finally, roses which are often the last variety to be placed in a large display may be liable to snap at the base of the head even though the lower part of the stem is sturdy. The correct use of support wiring can make their placement easier and the end results more dependable.

FOAM BLOCKS

The one product that is essentially different with dried flowers is the type of foam used. The foam for fresh flowers must readily absorb and hold water, whereas the foam for dried flowers needs to be strong enough to support the stems but not too resistant for fragile stems to be inserted without breaking. When purchasing blocks of dry foam, ensure that they are made of materials that are environmentally friendly.

GLUE GUNS, PAINT AND RIBBONS

Because using dried flowers to decorate hats and mirrors and to create collages is such a rewarding activity, a glue-gun is indispensable. The guns work by heating sticks of glue which melts and can be squeezed out of the nozzle. The glue dries very quickly and holds fast. Glue guns should not be used by children as the glue is very hot if accidentally touched and can cause blistering on the skin. Always have a bowl of cold water nearby.

Spray paint is also used more in dried flower work – not only for colouring plant material but also for changing the appearance of baskets or containers. Gold, bronze, silver and white are the most useful, especially for Christmas displays. Seed-cases or leaves, such as poppy and eucalyptus, can also be painted and then given a light spray for a glittering or frosted effect.

Raffia and twine can be used as ties for fresh or dried flowers but the choice of ribbons for fresh flower bouquets is limited by their need to be

The equipment needed for dried flower displays is minimal – but do buy a good hot glue gun.

water resistant. With dried flowers the options are much wider. As well as the usual fabric ribbons there are numerous types and colours made of paper or with wired edges. It is worth using good quality, expensive ribbons if the display is to last a long time. But, very economical ties and bows can be made from plaited leaves (maize leaves are ideal), or strips of leftover furnishing fabric. A fabric stiffener is useful when making big bows.

LOCATION STYLE AND CHARACTER

location and light

Having taken the trouble to produce or acquire quality dried flowers it is important to understand the rules of displaying them to best effect, so that the right flowers are used for the right situations. When selecting the type of plant material to use in a particular location consider the amount of direct light the display will receive, the humidity levels, the distance and angle from which the arrangement will be viewed, and the likelihood of disturbance (for instance in busy reception areas) or accidental damage from children and pets in the home. The interior design style of the location will also dictate the mood or theme of the display and will in turn influence the chosen plant material, container and style of arrangement.

Flowers in a domestic or commercial situation may last for a long time if they are left undisturbed but their appearance will deteriorate as they fade, become dusty or are accidentally damaged. Choosing the right flowers for the right location ensures that a display is attractive and eyecatching from the start and maintains its visual impact for a long time.

(opposite page) Brown, cream and yellow varieties from Australia, the Far East and South America can withstand the effects of strong sunlight for a long time.

Dried flowers are not 'everlasting' in normal conditions. It is true that sealed in the dry and dark conditions of an Egyptian pyramid, larkspur petals held their colour for hundreds of years… but no one was able to enjoy looking at them.

Most living plants depend for photosynthesis on the green chlorophyll in the leaves, buds or stems. There is nothing that can be done to prevent the chemical reaction caused by light shining on the chlorophyll, and the speed of fading is directly related to the intensity of the light and the length of exposure to it. It must be accepted that the natural green of any dried plant material will fade in time. Even larkspur with its long lasting petal colour, will show its age when the stem and the green tinge on the tips of the buds starts to pale.

Dried displays are often chosen because of their comparative longevity, so the aim must be to keep the flowers looking good for as long as possible.

▌ CHOOSING FLOWERS FOR BRIGHT SPOTS

When designing a display for a bright, well-lit location, you have several options:

1 Use any colours desired, but accept that the green items (unless dyed) will need to be replaced after a few months to maintain a fresh colour.

2 Omit grasses (except those cut at the golden stage) and other flowers on which green leaves, buds or seed-pods are dominant, such as *Carthamus*, *Nigella* and *Solidago*.

3 Select flowers with strong initial petal colour – they will last the longest. *Helichrysum* are excellent

for this (except perhaps the pale pink), as are *Limonium sinuatum*, *Achillea*, dark blue larkspur, dark pink or red peonies, lavender and red roses.

4 Use pale, neutral or brown plant material and put the emphasis of the design on form and texture. There is a surprisingly wide choice available – carline thistles, poppies, maize cobs and golden oats as well as exotic stems and seed-heads and many of the Australian varieties. The grey-leafed foliage of sage and eucalyptus is also useful.

5 Introduce deep-dyed items such as burgundy honesty, terracotta *Carthamus* or preserved green foliage as background material and integrate them with the natural-coloured varieties. (Note that it is very difficult to produce dyed material that looks a natural green – partly because there are so many subtle shades of green in nature.)

Generally it is better to avoid sunny locations for dried flowers in the home – windowsills and conservatories are better adorned with fresh flowers or plants which positively benefit from the sunlight. Internal walls, roof-spaces, beams, fireplaces, dressers and the spaces over kitchen units are all much more appropriate for dried flowers. Use them to brighten dark locations that are unsuitable for houseplants – alcoves, internal hallways or spaces under stairs. Here the green grasses, honesty, *Carthamus* and *Nigella* can be used to best effect, with highlights created by white *Achillea ptarmica*, *Anaphalis* and carline thistles.

Sometimes, however, people welcome the faded antique look that comes with time. The mellowness of ageing hop bines can be appropriate to the character of an old building!

location and humidity

Dried flowers are ideally suited to modern centrally heated environments and all will maintain their colour and form best in dry situations. The responses to a damp atmosphere vary according to the structure of the plant material but the effects are three-fold.

First, non-woody plant material – petals, buds, soft leaves and fleshy stems – will absorb atmospheric moisture. Sometimes, in the case of roses and peonies, this can be beneficial, softening the petals and allowing them to open out thus enlarging the bloom. But, generally when stems soften it is detrimental because either the stem tips bend over (as with *Amaranthus paniculatus*) or the flower-heads droop (as with *Helichrysum*). The flowers most at risk are those picked at the bud or early flowering stage because their stems are still young. Grasses, plants picked for their seed-pods and naturally woody species can tolerate higher humidity levels. Dried hop bines are brittle to handle and it is positively beneficial to leave them in a damp atmosphere for a few hours, or spray them with a fine mist of water, to soften the leaves and flower cones. They are then easier to hang as garlands and will dry out again quickly.

Second, when humidity levels are high or slight dampness is persistent (such as in poor storage conditions or when a dense, solid item has not been properly dried) mould will develop. Some minor forms of mould that have developed during storage can sometimes be brushed off or will naturally disappear when exposed to dry air but usually the musty smell of the mould is unpleasant and the flowers are best disposed of.

A bathroom picture framed in a manner appropriate to its subject with sea holly, sea lavender and dark blue Provence lavender.

Third, colour – particularly green – tends to be leached out of the flowers faster in a damp atmosphere or when humidity levels fluctuate.

■ CHOOSING FLOWERS FOR A DAMP ATMOSPHERE

The lesson to be learned from this is to ensure that the atmosphere is appropriate before installing a dried flower display. If the air is frequently damp, such as in a porch entrance or a bathroom, select strong-stemmed plant material or design the display in such a way as to ensure that all the flower-heads are well supported. Do not use varieties like *Amaranthus paniculatus* or *Agastache* whose design function is to give upright direction to an arrangement and whose character is lost if the stem tips bend over. Also, be careful with certain single-flowered peonies (such as 'Bowl of Beauty') or rose varieties, whose large petals can droop if too damp. Make sure weak-stemmed heads like *Anaphalis* are held in place by being either wired into clusters or closely surrounded by other plant material.

Do not be too horrified at the reaction of *Helichrysum* heads which close up into tight buds if accidentally splashed – they soon open out again when dry!

In the decoration of a bathroom, where blue colour schemes are often chosen, lavender, sea holly and sea lavender (*Limonium dumosum*) all survive happily. In the picture frame illustrated here the flowers have been simply tucked into place behind some old rope and fishing net.

busy locations

Dried flowers are usually more fragile than fresh ones. Stem tips can snap easily, leaves can crumble or break off, flower-heads can be damaged and seeds shed. Ideally, displays need to be located away from the passing traffic of people, inquisitive children or pets and also where they do not suffer from sudden draughts from windows or doors.

Where a location is unavoidably busy, ensure that strong-stemmed varieties predominate, that the display is compact in form, flower groups are securely wired into place and that the container is well balanced. Large dried flower displays in baskets can tend to be top heavy and may need to have the base weighted. Wall-mounted displays can usually be located above the level of disturbance.

In the home, cats can be attracted by certain floral scents and will dismantle a display that attracts them. Incorporating into the design some of the prickly items such as teasels, *Carthamus,* artichokes, cardoons, globe thistles – and especially carline thistles – can be a useful deterrent.

Traditional dried flowers tend not to be used as individual table centre decorations in restaurants. Well-secured arrangements of tough exotics or dried fruit are appropriate but delicate flowers cannot withstand the absent-minded attention of diners waiting between courses. However, at parties or wedding receptions, dried flowers make ideal displays because they can be prepared in advance and kept as souvenirs afterwards. Small wheat stooks, topiary trees and hand-tied posies can all be personalized to the occasion.

Dried flowers burn easily. In public places it is generally a requirement for insurance that all furnishings are fire-proofed to a satisfactory standard and dried flowers should not be overlooked. Fire-retardant sprays do an effective job without detracting from the appearance of a design.

In the home it is also necessary to take sensible precautions to ensure that the flowers are not in the vicinity of open fires or burning candles. When hanging bunches to dry, make sure they cannot drop on to a source of heat and ignite.

location and scale

A small posy or table centre, intended to be viewed from close quarters, can be intricately designed in such a way that individual flower-heads can be appreciated. Large-scale displays that are viewed from a distance, such as church pedestals, need to incorporate bigger individual items, such as peonies and artichokes, or to have individual varieties arranged in bold groups of several stems. Contrasts of texture, tone and colour are important and the stronger they are, the better the display will stand out from afar. However, it must be remembered that the detail of dark colours may be lost and appear as shadows. Yellow, orange and white flowers are always most visible from a distance and especially useful in locations that are not well lit (see the following chapter on designing with colour).

When creating big displays or ones located above eye level, keep stepping back to review the design from further away to ensure that the visual impact is right, and that focal flowers are correctly aligned to the angle of view.

■ HIGH CEILINGS AND BARNS

Simple trails of green hop bines are superb for decorating beams, marquees and archways and, in terms of value for money, they are unbeatable for the impact they give. Hanging baskets are excellent for rooms with high ceilings. Flat-backed wheat sheaves also provide simple forms, easily identifiable from a distance, and especially appropriate for barns and autumnal festivities.

The hop bine in this photograph was put up while still fresh and has dried in position, hanging gracefully along an old beam in a bedroom. Bells made of scented thyme were added for extra interest. When dry, a 3m (9ft) long hop bine weighs only 1kg (2lb) so needs little more support than a few nails and perhaps some string or thin wire. Commercially grown hops grow up a coir string which remains entwined with the stems after the bine has been cut down and can be used for tying the bine into place. The distinctive hoppy aroma emanating from the bine while it dries can be quite strong but soon fades.

Hops that are hung in place when fresh can be draped and twined into position and will dry to look natural and informal from close up or far away.

Fir cones, logs and bright orange Helichrysum *create the effect of warmth in an old fireplace.*

◼ DISPLAYS FOR FIREPLACES

The fireplace is often a focal point in a home and, even in a centrally heated room, people are naturally drawn towards the warmth and security that a hearth represents. In the winter when fires are lit (or switched on) the mantelpiece provides an ideal location for dried flowers – either a festive garland or a matching pair of pot designs or topiary trees. Take care that the flowers cannot be accidentally knocked and set alight.

Creating a simple fireplace display

The massive old brick and stone hearth featured on this page could no longer be used for open fires. Being located in a dining room, it was not the focal point and did not therefore need a dramatic eyecatching design. Imagery that reinforced the ideas of age and heat was all that was required. The huge pottery kettle (based on an old Welsh design) 'simmering' on a 'fire' of apple logs and 'lit' by flame-orange *Helichrysum* was all that was needed. It was a simple solution in contrast to the massed garden of flowers featured in the grand fireplace on the right hand page.

Considerations for fireplace displays

In the summer, when fires are no longer required, a living room still needs its point of focus and this is when many people choose to fill their hearth with flowers. The size and period style of the fireplace dictates the type of arrangement that is most suitable. Victorian and Edwardian grates, often framed by tiles, can be quite small. Instead of trying to fit a pre-filled basket into the grate, it is often easier to pack some dry foam into the space and insert the flowers directly into it. The flowers can then 'sprout' out from between the bars of the grate. The choice of flowers can either reflect the colour scheme of the room and the surrounding tiles or represent the colours of flame and smoke, with such varieties as yellow knapweed, Chinese lanterns, orange *Carthamus* and grey eucalyptus.

If a large traditional display is required, a container can be placed in front of the grate. Here, a symmetrical design may be called for but, if placed to one side, a carefully balanced asymmetrical display can be just as eyecatching although more challenging to create. Alternatively, you may want to consider a matching pair of free-standing wheat or flower stooks for an image of summer harvest.

Modern fireplaces which do not have a built-in grate are suitable for more unusual treatments, perhaps using a collection of containers and other objects (such as wooden fruit or carved birds). Some of the flowers could flow out of the opening and perhaps trail down over the hearth step.

It is always important to remember the angle of view. Displays in a hearth are invariably seen from above. Flowers therefore need to be placed to face the onlooker. Arrangements can look very different according to their angle of view so, ideally, create a display like this in situ – and stand back regularly to admire its progress.

creating style

Before starting to create a display in any location, think of the effect you are trying to achieve – formal or informal, refined or flamboyant, antique or modern. Creating style in a display is a process of selecting and combining together different elements, which have similarities of character, to create one overall impression.

■ ROMANTIC ENGLISH COUNTRY GARDEN STYLE

The choice of flowers is crucial here. They must be the old-fashioned varieties: larkspur, *Echinops*, peonies, roses, hydrangeas, lavender, love-in-a-mist, *Anaphalis* and *Achillea*. Poppies are valuable for their shape and contrast of texture, and eucalyptus varieties provide soft grey-green background foliage. Ornamental grasses, especially the millets, add freshness of colour. Exotic varieties and strong, hard geometric shapes look out of place here as do wheat and barley which are too agricultural in character and detract from the floral effect.

The style of design needs to be relaxed and not too formal – just like a herbaceous border in which the location of the plants has been carefully thought out to give a harmonious composition and each plant's character contributes towards the overall picture. Containers can range from baskets with handles to gardening trugs, elegant urns or hanging baskets.

A single basket would have been lost in this huge fireplace so instead the hearth was filled with a 'garden' of summer flowers. The colours were chosen to link with the rug in the foreground.

Herbaceous border effect
In the old stone fireplace illustrated here the image is of a herbaceous border in glorious full flower. Since the containers holding the bunches were only going to be visible at the very front, the method of supporting the flowers at the back of the arrangement needed only to be purely functional – in this instance, old wine boxes with their compartments intact provided an ideal low-cost support structure… albeit unsophisticated! Rectangular baskets of horizontal 'logs' provided the frontage.

Starting at the back with the eucalyptus, then larkspur and *Carthamus*, the flowers were grouped to as to reflect their natural character – the larkspur and *Echinops* 'grow' vertically while the hydrangeas and 'Dumosa' form bushy mounds. Most flowers were used in the same state in which they were dried, often still held together by their rubber bands and the bunches grouped together in twos or threes. The display was very simply and quickly constructed. (It used a lot of flowers… but one can afford to be extravagant if they have been grown and dried at home.)

*The strong shapes and
textures of a striking
bouquet complement the
simple decor.*

DRAMATIC, BOLD DISPLAYS

Although mostly purchased by women, dried
flowers have the scope to be strongly masculine in
imagery, especially if strikingly composed in bold,
simple, undecorated containers. Hop bines, large
artichokes, sturdy stooks of wheat and tall
bulrushes do not have a domestic or 'floral' image.
They are perfect for modern minimalist interiors as
well as being appropriate in offices, civic buildings,
and sports or health centres. Strong combinations
of simple textures and shapes can be dramatic and
eyecatching and retain their visual impact for a
long time. A collection of closed artichoke heads
tightly packed into a terracotta pot will look stylish
for months on a company board room table while
the metal vase of 'ting ting' shown on page 90
would grace any modern office reception area. In
pubs a hop bine strung over a bar or a sheaf of
barley hung on the wall will continue to imply
agricultural connections as the months go by.

Bold bouquets

Even in the home, carefully co-ordinated with the
fabrics of a room, a bouquet can have a masculine
rather than feminine character. The wall bouquet
shown here illustrates this well. The criteria for its
design were that it should be a wall decoration to
complement the decor of the dining room in an
old house. The furniture was all a rich, dark
mahogany with strongly striped curtains of
terracotta and dark red against walls of light ochre.
In a dining room the focus of attention is always
the table, and ornamentation elsewhere in the

room should complement the atmosphere of the decor without being too dominant. This display therefore needed to blend with the room colouring while drawing the eye with its strength of texture and boldness of form. A bouquet tied with raffia created a simple statement and needed no more than to be hung on a nail in the wall.

The varieties chosen were rich brown beech leaves as a background with red *Atriplex*, dyed terracotta *Carthamus* and dyed burgundy *Achillea filipendulina*. Stems of large-headed green Italian millet gave a freshness and softness of texture. Neutral-coloured poppies and twisted exotic stems provided contrasting texture and strong forms. Closed and open artichokes formed focal points towards the visual centre of the bouquet. The overall image created was not one of flowers but of complementary shapes and textures. (For guidance on how to make bouquets such as these, see the hints for gift bouquets on page 145.)

Similarly, the kitchen hanging basket on page 150 contains no flowers except the herb marjoram. Instead, it is packed with items that all have culinary associations – hops, chillies (on artificially wired and taped stems), poppies, mini pumpkins, cinnamon, fungi, dried fruit, wheat, millet, onion seed-heads and artichokes. Continuing with a culinary theme, the idea of the garden trellis illustrated here can be adapted for the kitchen where there are numerous other props that could be incorporated into a collage effect: wooden spoons, bunches of herbs, bags of spices, replica eggs and even pieces of kitchen equipment such as pastry cutters and napkin rings.

RUSTIC COUNTRY STYLE

Many people like to feature a more casual style of floral arrangement in a kitchen, studio or family room and reserve the more formal arrangements for living and reception rooms.

Rustic images are generally the easiest and cheapest to achieve. Natural, undyed grasses can be displayed on their own or in combination with other simple flowers in gold, orange, green and cream colour schemes. The flowers should not have too strong a garden association – *Carthamus,* cardoons, *Centaurea* varieties, common yarrow, wild marjoram and thyme, poppies, teasels and bulrushes are all appropriate.

Bunches can simply be hung from beams or picture hooks, stood in jugs or laid casually along shelves, the tops of dressers or kitchen units. The simpler the apparent method of display the better it will look. The overall display also needs to be loose in form, and not too neat or compact. Simple stooks or sheaves of grasses immediately summarize the countryside and can be tied with twine, raffia or strips of hessian.

Woven baskets (the older, the better), unglazed pottery or old jugs, weathered terracotta garden pots, trugs, old watering cans and wooden boxes make ideal containers. If they are chipped, dented, or roughly painted this can add to their appeal.

Fencing or trellis-work can form the background for wall displays and be made even more appropriate by the addition of rustic or gardening elements. In the photograph above a small hurdle woven of hazel was used as a basis for the design.

*This breathtaking bowl of
silica-dried peonies exudes
classical elegance and style.*

Initially the garden shed was ransacked to provide an assortment of possible ingredients for the scene – old tools and plant pots, bundles of raffia, balls of string, sacking, seed packets and plant labels. With the hurdle lying flat on a table, these items were placed in different positions until a satisfying composition was achieved. The elements were then glued or wired into position, and trimmed bunches of flowers fixed into the pots or tied into place with raffia. The varieties chosen represent a complete picture of the garden – the flower border, the herb bed and the vegetable patch – using roses, hydrangeas, poppies, sunflowers, yarrow, marjoram, sage, thyme, lavender, garlic, artichokes, maize and onion heads. Sacking and moss were used to link some of the elements and provide a different background texture in places. A pair of strong wire hanging loops were attached to the back.

▌ UPMARKET AND DOWNMARKET IMAGES

It is easy to downgrade a potentially good arrangement simply by the quality of plant material displayed. However, equally important in influencing whether a display has the right image are the inclusion or omission of particular varieties, the way in which they are presented and the choice of container.

Roses and peonies are not only expensive to buy but have an image of being upmarket. They immediately enhance an arrangement, which is why they are so important as focal flowers. Do not use them in informal displays of rustic character as

they will look out of place and be wasted. Other flowers, such as *Echinops*, carline thistles, hydrangeas and artichokes, have a certain aura about them, lending a natural air of sophistication to a display.

At the other end of the scale, *Helichrysum*, statice and sea lavender ('Dumosa'), used in excess, have acquired such a 'cheap and cheerful' image that some people will spurn them altogether. However, used discreetly and with careful placement they can be invaluable for colour co-ordination and as subtle background fillers and thus enhance the most stylish display.

The clever use of dyed or painted elements can help to set off focal flowers and lengthen the visual life of a display, but avoid bright, garishly dyed flowers or grasses. These will downgrade anything other than a very modern and deliberate floral statement. For a refined look burnished antique gold is much more effective than bright, overly shiny glittery gold.

Think also about how you locate and set-off a display – the placing of a mat underneath or a wall-hanging behind, or the grouping of several items around it will mark out the display as worthy of attention (see the pictures on pages 99 and 129).

The fashion in containers can change surprisingly quickly. In some designs, the style of the container is as important as the flowers. A cheap basket or unsteady pot will ruin a display so, if the container is to be visible, make sure it is worthy of being seen. If a ready-made one is not entirely appropriate, try adapting it with alternative paint finishes or trimmings.

Bowl of peonies

The bowl of peonies photographed here would not look out of place in the most elegant of settings. The container could be a stemmed fruit bowl, a china soup tureen or perhaps a silver rose bowl. The blooms were all dried in silica to preserve their characteristic full-blown size. Four varieties are illustrated – the light pink 'Sarah Bernhardt', the cream 'Duchesse de Nemours', the dark pink 'Monsieur Jules Elie' and an old-fashioned dark red *Paeonia officinalis*.

To create this effect, cut the peonies before they open into full flower when most of the central petals have unfurled but while the outer petals are still concave, not convex. Trim the stems to about 10cm (4in) in length. Sprinkle a layer of silica crystals in the bottom of a large plastic box and place the peony heads so that they do not touch one another. Using a spoon, carefully fill the spaces between the petals with the silica crystals so that the shape of the blooms is maintained. Continue to fill the box until the heads are completely hidden. Cover and put in a dark, dry place for a couple of weeks. When dry, gently remove each flower, shaking out the crystals. If they are not to be used at once in an arrangement, store in a dark, dry place – the petals are brittle and will re-absorb moisture very quickly if left in a damp atmosphere. Try drying a few leaves as well to add to the display.

To arrange the flowers into an open bowl like this, pack the container with dry foam and secure it in place with pot tape. Insert the flowers so that they form a dense mound. A selection of garden roses dried in silica could be similarly arranged.

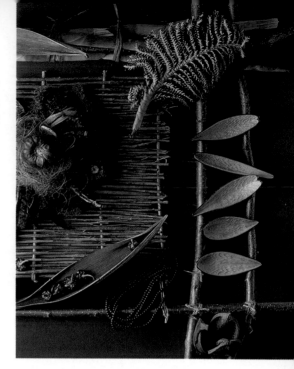

The products of four continents are represented in this collage, but the overall impression is African.

■ HISTORIC OR NATIONAL ASSOCIATIONS

Each era and each country has its own style, and floral displays can reflect this imagery without necessarily having to use items of antique value or from a specific country of origin.

Georgian elegance

The style of the Georgian era is well expressed by ornate swags and garlands and by Grecian-style urns overflowing with flowers and fruit. It was an era when, throughout Europe, floral decoration was everywhere – on porcelain, on plaster moulds, sculpted in marble, carved on wood, printed on fabrics and painted in oils. The imagery was sumptuous – fruit, flowers, birds, insects, combined with classical references to music, art and literature – against interior colour schemes of cream and pastel. Today, we have all the means to replicate these images and can make fabulous garlands of peonies, hydrangeas, larkspur, dried fruit and exotic leaves, gilding them in gold or paint sprays for a special effect. These look glorious over mirrors or mantelpieces and as wall hangings. Poppies, wheat, dried fruit and exotics sprayed with a dull gold are excellent with antique furnishings. Other surface coatings, such as 'distressed' matt finish pastel colours (like Wedgwood blue or dull ochres), blend well with period interiors. Containers need not be priceless antiques as long as they have certain essential characteristics. There are plenty of very good replica stone urns, vases, carved wooden pieces and ornate metalwork available.

An element of Georgian imagery has been captured in the wall display featured on page 146 – the gold and cream colour scheme, the use of swags of fabric, the cream peonies, gilded poppies and clusters of artificial fruit.

The traditional Dutch flower paintings illustrated imaginative combinations of flowers which would not naturally be blooming in the same season, for example, tulips and delphinium. With dried flowers, such combinations are easy to reproduce because seasonality is not a problem.

Victorian posies

One of the floral images of the Victorian era is of hand-held posies framed in lace and composed of concentric rings of different flowers, probably including *Alchemilla*, lavender, and, of course, roses. Such images are easy to replicate (see page 143 for the making of hand-tied bouquets).

Impressions of Africa

It is interesting how the collage above is so distinctly reminiscent of Africa when its ingredients are from so many other places – India, South America, the Far East and Europe. Its mood is generated largely by the earthy colouring – brown, terracotta and dark red – and the collection of exotic dried forms. Dried beans have been threaded into necklaces that look tribal, an image reinforced by the arrow-head form of the hard brown leaves and the spear-like stems of *Assegai* as well as the canoe shape of the light brown *Canoinha*. There is a nest in a jungle of moss and coconut fibre (see also page 88).

New England checks

Images of America, especially New England, are epitomized in floral displays by the addition of checked ribbons, patchwork dolls, and simple carved and painted wooden fruit and hearts. The Thanksgiving theme is always important with wreaths and table-centre designs made of dried fruit, mini pumpkins, nuts, herbs, wheat, oats and especially maize cobs.

Scandinavian minimalism

The minimalist and clean cut image of modern Scandinavian decor can be achieved by plain wooden, pottery or glass containers of single species, emphasizing form and texture. The seed-heads – 'Hen and chicken' poppies, teasels, honesty, Chinese lanterns – as well as many of the grasses are useful for this. Bundles of birch twigs, which are as evocative of Northern Europe as twisted willow is of Japanese floral art, can be left plain or painted white, perhaps with a hint of silver frosting at the right time of year.

seasonal character

Seasonal character can be created by concentrating on colours or varieties that have specific associations or by introducing extra props that have particular imagery.

SPRING

Each season has a distinct character of light and a predominance of particular colours. The light in spring is soft and this affects the way we see the colours. Spring is associated with the lime-green of new foliage, the yellow of daffodils and the lilac and blue shades of violets, bluebells and hyacinths. Many of these spring flowers are very difficult to air-dry successfully because they are fleshy and so cannot be used (though experimenting with silica is always worthwhile with tulips, hellebores and narcissi.) Instead, spring can be represented by its typical colours – the combination of the lemon *Helichrysum* or *Achillea* 'Moonshine' with light blue larkspur is always successful, and can be complemented by young green grasses such as *Phalaris* and *Bromus*.

Another familiar floral image of spring is the country basket planted with primroses or miniature daffodils and packed around with fresh moss. This can be recreated in dried flowers by echoing the colours and composition – 'planting' the stems in groups of varying heights and creating rosettes of leaves that 'grow' out of either cushion or flat moss. It is sometimes possible to obtain primrose baskets with a bent wood handle that were traditionally made from hazel by travelling country folk.

In the spring design illustrated here a different approach has been taken. The image of spring is concentrated in the bird's nest, hidden at the base of (what can be interpreted to be) last seasons' bulrushes with a few dried 'autumnal' leaves still around. New growth is represented by fresh green moss and the young stems and leaves of the grass *Setaria viridis*. Flowers of garden origin would have

Even though the varieties used are not those traditionally associated with spring, the presence of the bird's nest confirms the seasonal theme of the arrangement.

looked inappropriate but the colour of spring is hinted at by a few sprigs of yellow tansy and the delicate papery flowers of *Astrantia*. The design is contained in a plain plastic planting bowl packed with dry foam, which has been concealed by a circle of miniature bales of hay, bound together on the outside by rough jute twine. For fun, some little chocolate Easter eggs have been placed in the nest.

These vibrant flowers for a
bright location are in
individual vases so any that
fade can be easily replaced.

dealing with dried flowers. Here the lime green of the fabric is set against a lilac background. It would be impossible, without resorting to dyed colours to replicate this green and any other green shade could easily look dull against it. Remembering also the important fact that dried flowers will fade quickly in direct light, flowers were deliberately chosen for this display that were not reliant on green for their effect. Vases made of reconstituted stone were chosen to complement the flaked paint of the old metal garden table; a single variety was arranged simply in each vase. Lavender blue larkspur, dark blue lavender and a soft lilac hydrangea head provided the colour link to the painted background and the blue pattern on the fabric, but attention is focused on the sun-burst of golden *Craspedia*.

An alternative image of summer is of dry parched scenery, for which the Australian varieties are ideal with their subtle desert-like colours and woody forms. In the illustration on page 95, the containers used were of simple whitewashed pottery that had been deliberately cracked and broken – for good artistic reasons! The pots were closely grouped and the flowers allowed to flow out and mingle together. Shrubby *Banksia* flowers, yellow drumsticks and kangaroo paw, creamy sago and *Verticordia browni*i, as well as brown grass heads and *Rosa de Tefe* were used. Cassia sticks and flat slices of large *Banksia* heads were added for their contrasting shapes. The overall composition was completed with a selection of large smooth gourds, dried bean pods and some rough-textured plates.

■ SUMMER

Images of summer are easy to achieve with baskets of riotous colour. Summer sunshine is intense, with the colour emphasis on strong pinks, powerful blues, and bright whites. Summer greens are rich and dark. As in nature, a summer colour scheme can accommodate some quite shocking colour combinations – fresh yellows being set against pink, and lilac against red. The choice of varieties is extensive but it must include a predominance of flowers rather than seed-heads (which will tend to

look autumnal). The style of display can be full or loose, formal or informal. The fireplace illustrated on page 101 encapsulates summer with its lush 'herbaceous border' of flowers.

It has already been mentioned that conservatories are not the ideal location for dried flowers, but it is possible to create the image of a bright sunny garden room with the right containers and a vibrant colour scheme.

Bright green is such an important colour to represent the freshness of spring and summer but it is not always an easy colour to work when

AUTUMN

It is in this season that dried flowers come into their own, when flowers in the home are hanging to dry, apples and nuts are being picked, and fruits are being preserved and stored ready for winter.

Displays are often required for church festivals and Thanksgiving celebrations with autumnal images of nature's bounty – baskets of fruit, nuts, seeds and the all-important wheat and oats – and of the harvest safely gathered in. In the countryside colours are turning to golden yellows, oranges, terracotta, dark reds and browns, shades that are amply supplied by golden wheat and oats, *Carthamus, Helichrysum,* sunflowers and maize cobs.

The illustration shows a typical harvest festival collection. Inspired by the famous English poet John Keats in his 'Ode to Autumn', the display incorporates many literary references; the poem mentions the sun (hence sunflowers) plus fruit, vines (in this case a piece of hop bine), hazel nuts, swathes of corn, poppies and the reaper's hook. They are all combined together in a still-life composition which uses a wooden apple box, an old flour measure and some garden pots. For harvest festival displays, flower arrangers collect whatever is readily available at the time – and since early autumn is the season for picking sunflowers and apples, they are included here as fresh, not dried, items.

Fresh and dried flowers can combine well in a harvest festival composition.

Mixing fresh and dried flowers

It is often not considered possible to mix fresh and dried flowers together as in the harvest display on the previous page. This is partly because the fresh flowers' need for water restricts their versatility but, more often, the problem is that the bright colouring of fresh-cut flowers is too great a contrast to the subtlety of the dried ones. (The fresh therefore visually dominate the dried flowers.) Here it is shown how the two can be successfully and dramatically combined, with each retaining its integrity. The sunflowers and the stook of wheat complement one another perfectly, one relying on brightness of colour, the other on form and texture. Similarly, the smooth form of the golden courgettes complements but does not dominate the interesting texture of the dried maize cobs. The shiny red apples show up against the matt terracotta jug behind.

The choice of green wheat was important here; it is vibrant enough to stand out against the dark green background leaves of the sunflowers. The more logical seasonal choice of golden wheat would, in fact, have dulled the overall effect.

Dried flowers can thus be successfully used in combination with fresh ones provided that the varieties are carefully selected and cleverly used, and that the dried materials are in prime condition with the best possible colour preserved.

WINTER

In Europe and North America, winter floral themes have often concentrated on the Christmas imagery of green, red and glittering gold – with holly, ivy, conifer branches, cones and decorative ribbons. More recently, alternative styles have been promoted with branches of white-painted birch twigs, silver, grey and blue colourings (reflecting the colder light of winter), or rich, warm combinations of antique gold and dark burgundy. Even with dyeing, it is difficult to achieve good dark green foliage with dried flowers so these alternative fashion trends are welcome – and dried flowers have extended the range of floral possibilities with decorative paint and spray finishes and the use of exotic varieties, spices and dried fruit.

The Christmas table-centre project on page 137 uses a traditional colour scheme of red, gold and white with red roses, *Solidago*, carline thistles, gold poppies, white larkspur, *Nigella* and glycerined green beech leaves. In contrast, the winter door ring on page 136 uses tones of grey, white and orange with eucalyptus, *Anaphalis*, sea lavender, and gold poppies, plus trailing raffia strings of cinnamon, Chinese lanterns and orange slices.

Floral displays of dried flowers designed purely to express the theme of winter can achieve great impact by the clever use of subtle tones and bold textures. The brick fireplace on page 100 simply uses the hot colours of orange and scarlet *Helichrysum* to represent the glow of a fire among apple logs.

The snow scenes of winter outdoors, can be captured by the textural combination of all the white flowers – *Anaphalis, Achillea ptarmica*, white statice, 'Dumosa', *Gypsophila*, carline thistles and natural reindeer moss. It is great fun to allow the imagination to run riot with such scenes and, if creating a large display, to incorporate some unexpected props – a knitted scarf perhaps, or a carol-singer's music and lantern. On a personal note, I consider it a challenge to make someone smile when they see an exhibition display or still-life composition that I have made – and it may be only a little detail that is needed to achieve this.

The arrangement here was created to encapsulate winter. It used a frosted green glass vase into which the dry foam was wedged. (If, in such a vase, you find the foam remains visible through the glass, use chalk to add to the frosted effect.) Buttermilk coloured poppy heads were combined with white painted birch stems, larch twigs and cassia sticks. The leaves of the dark green *Eucalyptus stellulata* were given a faint spray of white paint to achieve the effect of a dusting of snow. The composition was begun with the dominant spiral of poppies, followed by the birch twigs, and then the eucalyptus. The brown cassia sticks were used to give a touch of warmth and to strengthen the vertical lines of the composition. The larch twigs were added last to lessen the formality of the arrangement. Dried pomegranates, with a hint of antique gold, provide a delicate finishing touch.

A display like this may only be required for a limited period but, if safely packed away for the summer months along with the other Christmas decorations, it will give pleasure year after year.

COLOUR AND COMPOSITION

IN DESIGN

a new approach

The purpose of this chapter is to look closely at how dried flower displays can be designed to co-ordinate with fabrics and interior colour schemes. This involves the challenge of selecting the right flowers that not only link with a colour scheme but whose texture, size and form also complement one another as a collection. Also to be considered is the artistic and technical skill of combining them to create a successful composition. These design principles are explained and then illustrated by reference to specific projects.

The quality of colour associated with dried flowers has improved dramatically with the advent of kiln drying. The palette of colours now available to floral designers is not as vibrant as that offered by fresh flowers (dried flowers are always more subtle and muted even when superbly preserved), but the exciting ways in which dried flowers can be combined together and presented more than compensates for this.

Dried flowers, by their nature, are never used without the intention that they last for a worthwhile period of time. Reconciling the fact that the flowers will gradually fade, with the need to retain long-term visual impact, is the skill of a good floral artist. In creating a design that will be appropriate to its surroundings and be a delight to look at, the designer needs to work not only with strong forms and textural contrasts but with the clever choice and placement of colour.

▪ CREATING VISUAL IMPACT

By using strong colour contrasts, and sometimes shocking the eye with unexpected combinations, it is possible to create displays that have a powerful, impact, thereby compensating for the quieter individual tones of the blooms.

Many flower arrangers, familiar with fresh flowers, find it difficult to adapt to arranging dried flowers. They can be daunted by the lack of green leaves on which they depend for background volume. In fresh flower work, green foliage is often used for its neutrality to offset the colour of the blooms. To arrange dried flowers successfully it is

necessary to make a virtue of necessity – to use the absence of foliage as a positive factor and to delight in placing colour against colour without green 'getting in the way'.

A different approach is also needed to the building up of a dried display. Because foliage is so crucial to the design of fresh displays it is usually the first element to be placed in position, often followed by the focal flowers and then in-filled with other varieties. With dried flowers, other considerations have to be taken into account – the sheer quantity of stems being used, the need for long-term support, the fragility of the heads, and so on – and these factors dictate the way an arrangement is built up. The focal flowers are often not positioned until the very end.

understanding colour

It is not the intention here to delve deeply into the science or psychology of colour but a brief summary of the principles may be useful. For those who do not trust their instinct on such matters it may initially be helpful to refer to the colour wheel on the following pages.

There are three primary colours – red, yellow and blue – which stand alone and cannot be created by mixing other colours. By combining these colours in pairs, the intermediates of orange, green and indigo are made. The opposite or complementary of red is green –the mixture of yellow and blue. The opposite of yellow is indigo – the mixture of red and blue and the opposite of blue is orange – the mixture of red and yellow. Other colours are achieved by the addition of either white, to create tints, such as pink, the addition of grey to create tones, such as slate blue, or the addition of black to create shades, such as crimson. These colours will always be softer on the eye because they are less pure. Achromatic or neutral colours are ones which are not readily associated with any of the colours on the wheel: black, white, grey, beige and stone.

COMPLEMENTARY COLOURS

A colour will stand out most strongly when set against its complementary colour on the opposite side of the colour wheel. But there are also colours that clash strongly, such as orange and pink, or lilac and bright red. Such dynamic contrasts need to be carefully handled because, in excess, their effect can be too harsh and therefore ultimately unpleasant or tiring to look at. There is no such thing as a bad colour combination, but it can be inappropriate or out of place. However, nature can often successfully display colour combinations that would be unheard of in clothing, and with dried flowers the subtlety of colouring is such that the overall effect can be eminently dramatic and eyecatching. (It is important to remember that the more dramatic the shape, colours or textures of an arrangement are at the beginning, the longer its visual impact will last – so be adventurous.)

COLOUR AND MOOD

People react to colours both physically and emotionally. Yellows, oranges and reds are 'advancing' hot colours which catch the attention, whereas greeny-blue to violet colours are perceived as 'receding' or cool. Colours are thus associated with different moods. Red is aggressive, powerful and signifies danger, but is also romantic, being the colour of blood and the heart. Blue is the colour of the intellect – calm, cool and reflective. Yellow can be harsh and aggravate the emotions. Green is considered to be balanced and at ease with itself and has obvious associations with the natural world.

The use of colour to create mood or image is everywhere – green in the logos of companies wishing to stress an environmental awareness, warm dark reds in restaurants to promote moods of well-being, soft peaches and pinks in hotel rooms to make guests feel relaxed and at ease, and harsh bright colours in fast food outlets which do not want their customers to sit around for too long. Floral designs for such surroundings need to be equally sensitive to the mood they are to create.

MAKING COLOUR STATEMENTS

Once familiar with the principles of colour, it is easier to understand why some colour combinations work better than others; it is therefore possible to design not only a collection of flowers that co-ordinate together but a complete style statement whereby flowers, container, and background are in harmony with the whole room.

The arrangement on the left hand page illustrates how using these principles creates drama. The idea is simple enough – Chinese lantern heads glued on to wheat stalks and contained in a plain pot. A frill of open lanterns and reindeer moss encircles the rim and there is a band of preserved burgundy-dyed oak leaves around the base of the stalks.

The drama comes from the simplicity of the form – the vertical thrust of the stems and pointed lanterns – and the contrasts in colour. The bright orange is offset by the complementary blue-green of the stems. The redder colour of the berries contained in the open lanterns is reflected in the rich, matt, terracotta-red paint of the pot. (A shiny pot would have detracted from the sheen on the lanterns and a plain terracotta garden pot would have been too dull in colour.) The oak leaves pick up the shadow colour of the pot and lanterns.

Against an inappropriate background all this fine-tuning of colour would have been lost. Here the deliberate choice has been a rich royal blue – the exact opposite of orange on the colour wheel (see the following pages) and therefore the strongest and most dramatic background possible to show off the display. The use of two pieces of driftwood as a stand for the pot was a quirky addition but nevertheless gives the arrangement even more status, demanding that it is noticed.

In the home there may not be the opportunity or the need for such dramatic pieces and the desire is likely to be for calm and harmony, so colour needs to be used more gently. There is also not usually the luxury of choosing the background to match the flowers – it tends to be the other way round.

colour wheel

This colour wheel has been specifically designed as an aid to the selection of dried flowers. The colours may not be strictly accurate in scientific terms but have been approximated to the flowers most commonly available. Some of the varieties which correspond most closely to the given colours are listed additionally.

Flowers colours are incredibly subtle and complex and so are difficult to categorise. For instance, *Limonium suworowii* has blue tones in its pink colour but is not as dark as magenta; the lavender blue larkspur has pink tones in it but is more blue than lilac; the seed-pod of *Nigella damascena* has stripes of mid-green and magenta/burgundy; and some hydrangeas contain so many colours that they could almost fill the spectrum from pink to lime green (which is why they are so useful and popular.)

Remember that this colour wheel is only to be used as a guide. Each individual sees colours in a different way and what may appear a harmonious blend to one may be unattractive to another.

Delphinium (pink)
Gypsophila or *Dumosa* (dyed pink)
Helichrysum (silver rose)
Peonia 'Sarah Bernhardt'
Rosa 'Kiss'

Helichrysum (dark pink)
Liatris spicata
Origanum vulgare
Paeonia 'Jules Elie'
Rosa 'Europa'

Cynara sp
Limonium sinuatum (lilac)

Centaurea cyanus
Delphinium (dark blue)
Echinops
Hydrangea sp
Lavandula sp
Limonium sinuatum (blue)

Bay leaves
Eucalyptus sp
Panicum violaceum
Peony and rose leaves
Triticum sp

Carthamus (in bud)
Grasses (in flower)
Lunaria biennis
Millets
Nigella orientalis

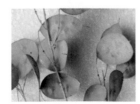

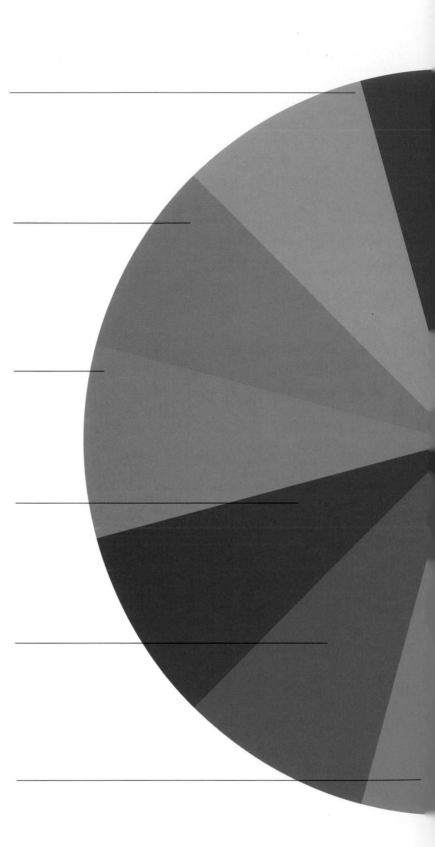

Rosa 'Mercedes' (bright red)
Rosa 'Jaguar' (dark red)
Helichrysum (scarlet)
Paeonia 'Rubra Plena (dark red)

Achillea ptarmica (dyed peach)
Helichrysum (salmon)
Limonium dumosum (dyed peach)
Limonium sinuatum (apricot)

Carthamus tinctorius
Helichrysum (orange)
Physalis

Achillea filipendulina
Centaurea macrocephala
Craspedia globosa
Helichrysum (gold)
Rosa sp
Zea mais

Achillea 'Moonshine'
Helichrysum (lemon)

Alchemilla mollis
Solidago

co-ordinating colours with fabrics

In recent years there has been a huge increase of interest in interior design. A wealth of home magazines promote different styles of furniture and fabulous ranges of materials, DIY outlets are prospering and, more than ever before, people are wanting to create co-ordinated interiors. Flowers are often the finishing touch of such schemes. Fresh flowers can have seasonal connotations and may be limited to seasonal colours, but dried flowers can contribute to a room's decor throughout the year. With the range of colours and varieties now available it is possible to co-ordinate with any colour scheme or any design style.

If a floral display is to co-ordinate in the long term with the decor, the flowers need careful selection. All too often, the mistake is made of choosing flowers that blend impeccably with a room's carpet, wall or fabric colours and the resultant effect is one of camouflage. A flower arrangement should always be considered as a focal point, attracting attention. The knack, therefore, is to be aware of the principal colours but to select some flowers that are brighter, some that are darker and maybe to put in a few sharp contrasts in order to make the display stand out against the other furnishings.

STYLING A DISPLAY

The size of a room and the style of its decor will dictate whether a display should have clean and simple lines, be bold and dramatic, or be complex and intricate. In a room with ornate or strongly patterned furnishings a simple display with clean

lines may be needed, but in a Georgian period interior a rich collection of varieties might be more appropriate. A stylish, minimalist monotone display could blend well in a modern room but, alternatively, something bold, dramatic and colourful might be used to attract attention. All the time, the scale of the display must be borne in mind in relation to the room so it is neither too over-powering nor too diminutive.

Some displays can be designed to include fabric to complement a room's furnishings. This fabric can be anything from rough sacking (see the garden fence project on page 103) or gold-patterned muslin as in the swag on page 146. Swags for the living room or bedroom can have curtain or upholstery fabric incorporated into them and wedding garlands of dried flowers can include some of the bride's or bridesmaids' dress fabric. Bows can be made into finishing touches for pots or basket arrangements, although a fabric stiffener may be needed to ensure they hold their shape.

The varieties selected pick out the darker tones and highlights of the furnishings and are not simply an exact colour match.

DRAMATIC DISPLAY OF MUTED COLOURS FOR A BEDROOM

The example illustrated is of a peaches and cream colour scheme. The brief was to create a decoration to hang on the wall above a wooden bedstead. The effect needed to be dramatic and unusual but also softly rustic, so it was decided to make some delicate garlands and twine them along a branch of twisted willow (*Salix matsudana* 'Tortuosa').

The usual mistake that people make with such a colour scheme is to try to select an exact match, and what they actually achieve is a soft but indistinct blend of varieties that camouflage themselves beautifully against the fabric. The photograph with sample bunches laid across the two pillows illustrates this point. Here, white *Gypsophila*, natural 'Dumosa' and *Achillea ptarmica* (dyed peach) provide just the right colours to link with the fabric and are shown wired together in a spray on the pillow. The effect is pretty and delicate but unexceptional. A more powerful effect – equally appropriate to the fabric – can be achieved by introducing not only stronger colours, but also contrasting textures and shapes. The collection of additional bunches on the left includes natural undyed *Achillea ptarmica*, plus dyed *Carthamus*, honesty and *Achillea filipendulina*, thus offering a bright eyecatching white and a range of darker burgundy and terracotta colourings. The rich tones of the salmon *Helichrysum* flowers provide warmth of focus as well as a link to the ochre wall colour. Natural green canary grass (*Phalaris canariensis*) gives freshness and balances the dyed colours. The varieties all complement one another as a harmonious group.

The varying character of these items dictated the way they were used in the construction of the design. Since the branch was naturally thicker at one end than the other, the three garlands needed to reflect this by being thicker towards the trunk and gradually trailing off towards the end of the twigs. However, even though they needed to look as if they were growing from left to right, they had to be made by starting at the finer end and being gradually built up. Beginning at the tip with the palest and most delicate flowers, the garlands were thickened by the gradual introduction of bigger concentrations of each variety, as well as the stronger colours and the bolder forms. The garlands were made using only reel wire to bind the stems together progressively, as shown by the spray in the photograph.

For added interest in the overall design, the garland for the top branch was made only of the white flowers, the garland on the lowest branch used just the soft peach and cream-coloured flowers and the central garland had the strongest, richest and warmest colours, using all the varieties. The garlands were all made separately, and then twined along the branches and secured into place.

Co-ordinating with fabric colours is
great fun – often leading to unusual
flower combinations that would not
otherwise have been considered.

MIXING DYED AND NATURAL VARIETIES IN A TRUG

To complement a fabric with a dominant colour or pattern, it is necessary to create floral designs that are capable of being equally eyecatching. Either the colours need to be strong or the compositional lines need to be powerful – or both.

The challenge in this example was to create a piece to co-ordinate with a strikingly embroidered Indian wall-hanging in earthy colourings of dark red, peach, beige and saffron yellow. It had silvery trimmings and was inset with small pieces of mirror, and was displayed against a background wall painted bright, golden yellow. The arrangement needed to sit on a glossy green wooden storage box.

By using the simple garden trug as a container it was possible to reflect the horizontal lines of the wooden box. However, the horizontal and vertical symmetry of the trug did not necessarily require the design to follow suit. In fact, deciding on an asymmetrical arrangement helped the overall impact of the display.

Choosing the colour scheme required patience and several trial combinations until the final selection was made. To stand out in this setting the colours and forms needed to be bold but with unusual contrasts. Bright or garish colours would have conflicted with the muted tones of the wall-hanging. Colours were needed that clashed – but subtly! The colour needed to be long lasting in this bright situation so it was best to avoid natural greens and to use some dyed elements.

The embroidery contained floral images in the daisy shapes but was by no means a floral pattern. Likewise, the display needed to be a collection of flower shapes without being 'flowery' in its effect.

Choosing the flowers

The *Achillea filipendulina* presented itself as a flower that accurately reflected the saffron yellow in the paint and the wall-hanging. Its shape, being so distinctly flat, could be used to emphasize the horizontal lines of the composition. The poppies, being native to India, were an obvious and authentic choice but also had the assets of bold shape, smooth texture and neutral colour in contrast to the other flowers. It was necessary for the composition to have a strong vertical element that did not detract from the main horizontal band of focal colour – green grasses were not appropriate with these arid earthy tones and none of the larkspurs were the right colour (they would also have been too floral) but the upright red *Amaranthus paniculatus* served the purpose well.

The pale peach and terracotta tones were picked up by the use of dyed *Achillea ptarmica* as a background filler. Peach and golden yellow do not usually sit happily together but more sense was made of this possible visual clash by adding the stems of dyed blue oats.

The use of complementary colours has already been mentioned but here is something closer to a 'split complementary'. A colour on one side of the wheel is not set against its direct opposite but against the two colours on either side of its direct opposite – in this instance, the violet blue against the greeny-yellow and the peachy-orange.

Although the blue oats linked to the silvery elements in the wall-hanging, if they had been the only blue variety they would have looked isolated. The large masses of blue-green hydrangea heads were used to reinforce the colouring of the oats while also reflecting the green of the painted box.

The focal flower

The crucial decision was the choice of focal flower. It needed to stand out in colour and shape. The rose was not an obvious choice at first but possessed the attribute of providing a distinctly floral shape against the other colour masses. Red roses would have been lost against the background. Bright yellow roses would have been dominated by the strong tones of the *A. filipendulina*. The bright, dark pink rose provided the answer, showing up well against the burgundy *Amaranthus*, linking beautifully with the hydrangeas and oats ('Europa' has lovely bluish-purple undertones), and complementing the yellow. It also clashed sharply with the peachy-orange *Achillea ptarmica*, thus ensuring it made its presence felt. The basket rim and handle were partly concealed by flowers to give a natural look, but the plain wood of the handle also helped to show up the roses as being important.

The composition

Although predominantly horizontal, the design needed height to link it to the wall-hanging. The tall *Amaranthus* stems on the left were balanced by a lower group on the right and also by the oats

projecting to the right-hand side. The large hydrangea on the far left was balanced by the smaller head in the mid right. The *A. filipendulina* and poppies were staggered in height to lead the eye down to the central mass of roses, thereby reinforcing the eyes' natural movement from left to right. The finishing touch to the scheme was the collection of dahlia heads in purple, pink, red and yellow, placed on the right hand side to balance the height on the left. The yellow heads were especially useful to link with the yellow *Achillea* and the wall behind the trug arrangement.

Because of the way that the colour and shapes are used, this display can maintain a visual impact over a long period of time. It does not distract the eye from the wall-hanging and yet it has its own integrity as a design. The two complement one another so unifying this area of the room.

harmony of composition

To achieve harmony, that is, for a display to be pleasing to look at, the composition must be balanced and the eye must be able to move freely around it, coming to rest each time on the intended focal points. On a larger scale, where a display is an important feature in a room (particularly in minimalist schemes), the positioning and shape of the display must likewise be in harmony with the whole scene.

■ CREATING BALANCE

To have visual balance, an arrangement must not be top heavy or lopsided or look as if it will overbalance. While creating the design, the arranger must be aware of where the visual centre of gravity lies and ensure that the visual 'weight' of bold elements is appropriately located. The strongest colours and largest forms are usually placed towards the base or, in symmetrical displays, towards the centre. Linear forms like the grasses or larkspur should all radiate from approximately the same point. (In the celebration swag on page 146 there are two focal points, created by the peony flowers and emphasized by the radiating stems of green *Amaranthus,* larkspur and poppy.)

In any painting or piece of sculpture the viewer is unconsciously led around the picture by the composition of the forms depicted and the lines or blocks of colour. The attention should be drawn back each time to the main subject matter. (When we learn to read books the eye is trained in certain ways and this can influence the way we 'read' compositions.) The same rules apply in floral art –

the attention should not be led away from the most important flowers or distracted by jarring elements. A good floral display should hold the attention for more than just a cursory glance – it should be intricate, or intriguing enough to be worthy of further study. A bland display, with nothing to excite the eye, will not provide lasting enjoyment. The composition of a wall display or

flat-backed arrangement, seen from only one direction, can be treated in some ways like a painting, but most arrangements, being three-dimensional, must be designed more like sculptures.

The wavy Limonium suworowii *and twisted maize leaves create visual movement, reinforcing the S-shaped style of the bouquet.*

CREATING MOVEMENT

Creating a feeling of movement or visual flow in a dried flower display is not as easy as with fresh flowers. Fresh flowers are naturally soft and curvaceous. The stems of dried flowers are invariably straight – simply from being hung up to dry – and, for the same reason, the heads are often perpendicular to the stem. Dried flower petals can also tend to have a crumpled look compared with the smoothness of fresh ones.

Dried flower material that is arched or smooth can be important in floral compositions, hence the popularity of twisted willow and some of the exotic varieties that have wavy or spiralled forms and sleek surfaces. (Remember this when cropping *Achillea filipendulina* and do not discard twisted or bent stems as they are artistically valuable.)

The trailing *Amaranthus caudatus* has a naturally flowing form which is ideal in pedestal displays or hanging baskets. The other variety invaluable for its graceful form is panicum millet: not only is it flexible and supple in itself when being handled but the weight of the seeds makes it softly arch over. The inclusion of this grass in a display can provide a welcome contrast to the rigidity of some other forms.

If the dried material is straight or formal, movement needs to be created in another way – by making the eye follow a route through the design. Patterns can be generated with the linear direction of stems or by the grouping of different colours or textures. The winter arrangement in the frosted green vase on page 111 is a good example. The white poppies physically form a spiral around the other vertical stems, leading the eye from the base around the back and up to the top. The arched twigs of larch also contrast with the straight birch stems and cassia sticks.

COMBINING PLANT MATERIAL SUCCESSFULLY

It is not only colours that will catch the attention, the eye will also be drawn to elements that are strong in scale or texture. These need to be balanced just as carefully as the colours and attention paid to the overall composition.

Imagine the example of a bouquet of red roses; combining them with something white to give a lift and something green as background is good policy, but the effect of putting white statice and green *Carthamus* with the red roses is totally different to using *Gypsophila* and *Nigella damascena*. The roses are the important focal flower and the function of any others in the bouquet must be to help show them up. The white of statice is too harsh and being bright it draws the eye away from the roses. The green of the *Carthamus* is appropriate, since it is a complementary colour to the red, but the size of the buds is too similar to the scale of the roses and therefore competes with them. The whole effect of the combination is therefore very jarring; the eye is unsettled, not knowing on which element it should rest.

The alternative combination is completely harmonious – the tiny *Gypsophila* flowers sparkle lightly against the red roses and the *Nigella damascena* is a perfect complement, its form being delicate and feathery in contrast to the rose petals; its colour combines an interesting blend of green and dark burgundy which links with the shadow colour of the petals.

The first, and most crucial challenge is therefore to select the right varieties to work with one another. The second challenge is to combine them together in a way that allows each to contribute towards the overall composition. Each chosen variety must serve a specific purpose – to provide focus, background, direction, texture or volume. Some varieties may fulfil more than one function. In a large display as many as nine different varieties may be needed with additional roles, providing contrast colour to the focal flowers, background filler, foreground filler, highlights or additional colour links. Using more than nine varieties may unnecessarily duplicate one of these functions and thereby risk making the arrangement look fussy. For the same reason, it is also not usually advisable to use two different colours of the same variety in one arrangement.

selection and design sequence

CREATING A LARGE FLAT-BACKED DISPLAY

In the finished example photographed on page 127 the project was to create a flat-backed display suitable for a side-table. It needed to match a fabric with an unusual and challenging colour scheme. The material depicted floral sprays in lime green, dark green, peach, cream, warm terracotta and burgundy-pink, against a lilac background streaked with dark blue – a combination of colours not usually associated with one another.

Choosing varieties

Sometimes it is difficult to know where to start in selecting flowers – it may be that the fabric pattern or room style suggests a certain flower, or that the fabric colours can only be reflected by particular varieties. Changing just one variety within the selection will influence the look of all the others. It is important to keep an open mind and try all sorts of combinations.

For the fabric illustrated, there was only one flower that could link with the background colour – the lilac statice. Pink and burgundy colours work well with lilac, so preserved and dyed oak leaves were chosen to provide the main structural background, with dyed *Carthamus* as the main filler. The pink larkspur was selected to give direction and height.

Deciding on shape

The fabric pattern suggested that the focal element should be a soft, round floral form; roses would be too small for the scale of the display, but peonies were ideal. (A strong architectural form like an artichoke or carline thistle would have been inappropriate.) The dark cerise-red peonies linked well with the fabric and with the lilac statice.

So far, the colour combinations were working well but the overall effect was quite dark. Silver-rose *Helichrysum* provided a lighter contrast against the peonies while linking with the light peach hues in the fabric. Hydrangeas provided more muted tones of soft lilac blue, their large heads also giving textural contrast and useful bulk as fillers. The fluffy *Anaphalis* was added to give soft highlights. The final crucial element in the selection was the frothy lime green *Alchemilla*. It fulfilled several important functions: providing another colour link to the fabric, giving an overall freshness to the display, adding a totally different and delicate texture, and being restful to the eye amid the other powerful colours. The lime green, since it is in direct contrast to the violet-reds, had a dramatic impact and very little of it was needed to achieve this effect.

When making a large display of several varieties it is always necessary to try different combinations of colours and varieties. This selection is warm and vibrant.

An alternative selection

The first selection of flowers works admirably, but it is by no means the only possibility. Personal preference and the availability of different varieties are obviously factors that influence the outcome of such a design. There might be a preference for a paler coloured display, there may not be any dark peonies available, or there may be a need to link with more blues in another part of the room. How would this influence the selection?

If the pink larkspur of the first selection is replaced with dark blue larkspur the effects are far-reaching – the dark burgundy colours can no longer dominate. The dyed honesty can be used as a background filler instead of the *Carthamus,* but the dark peony needs to be replaced with the cream 'Duchesse de Nemours'. The white *Anaphalis* is then no longer harmonious and the silver-rose *Helichrysum* is too pale. One solution is to veer towards a peach colouring and use the dyed *Achillea ptarmica* and salmon *Helichrysum.* The lilac statice, hydrangea and *Alchemilla* can all remain, fulfilling the same functions as before. The collection is nearly complete… but this lighter colour scheme is helped by the addition of another green element. The Italian millet (*Setaria italica*), provides the answer; it reinforces the freshness of the *Alchemilla* and can be used as background structure (in the same way that red oak was used in the first collection).

However carefully one selects the varieties and plans an arrangement, it is always necessary to keep an open mind because ideas may change as the display develops. Allow scope for spontaneity.

This alternative selection is cooler and more reserved than the first. Each variety reacts visually with the others. Changing just one requires a rethink of all the whole collection.

Choosing a container

Choosing a container is also important. If it is to be seen, it must complement the overall scheme. Here the colour and forms are powerful and a solid, stable container is appropriate. Being on a table, rather than at ground level, means that the container will be partly visible. A rectangular basket provides a good solid base of appropriate character to this collection of herbaceous species, its vertical slats being reminiscent of a garden fence. It needs to be firmly packed with dry foam that finishes slightly above the level of the rim, so that the flowers at the front and side can be placed at a lower angle to conceal the edge.

■ THE FLORAL ARTIST

Creating a floral display is like painting a still-life picture. Artists must work within the parameters of the canvas or paper whereas a floral designer has constraints of size or scale dictated by location. Both artists must understand the materials they are working with, have a palette of colours at their disposal and be driven by an image of what they want to create, but they must also be open to spontaneous inspiration as the design develops. Results can often be surprisingly satisfying.

The background structure of the display is built up first, ensuring that each variety is visually balanced within the composition.

Background structure

The first step (as with a painting) is to rough out the outline of the composition, to ensure that it is visually balanced. This is done with the plant material chosen to provide background structure; in the first selection, described above, this is the branches of red oak. It delineates the height and width of the display and small pieces of it can be introduced (now or later) into the foreground to balance the composition in three dimensions. In a display of symmetrical shape it is helpful to start off with the background being symmetrical, even if other flowers are to be grouped more naturally.

In an arrangement like this, it is a good idea to place the background flowers at an angle whereby they are leaning back slightly. Not only does this make the display physically more stable, but it helps provide room for all the other flowers to be placed in the foreground. If the back stems start off upright, the display will tend to look as if it is leaning forward. A conscious effort is needed when placing the foreground flowers to remember the angle from which they will be seen and to ensure that the central flowers face the viewer. For fireplaces or other displays placed at floor level, this angling of the background and focal flowers needs to be even more pronounced.

The second step (again, similar to a painting) is to fill in the background. The larkspur starts by echoing the function of the oak leaves, stressing height and width. Larkspur must be viewed from the side for full effect, so it needs to stand proud of other flowers. Being a linear form, the eye will be drawn along its lines and it is therefore important

that all the stems visually radiate from the same place – where the focal flowers are intended to be, towards the base of the display. The larkspur provides a dominant colour so it is helpful to the composition if the stems are grouped together and placed so that the eye can move from one group to the other. In this instance, the flow of colour is from the dominant centre back, down to the middle and lower right-hand side, but is balanced by a group on the extreme lower left-hand side. The larkspur firmly establishes the solid vertical emphasis of the design, reflecting the vertical slatted pattern of the container.

The background filler, *Carthamus*, is placed next so as to support the structural work of the red oak and to offset the pink larkspur. To do this effectively it needs to be in groups of several stems and to be positioned in close proximity to the larkspur without concealing it. *Carthamus* can be viewed from the side or full-face, so is also useful in the middle foreground.

Painting with flowers

An artist who has a certain colour on a brush will use that colour where it is needed throughout a picture rather than continually changing from one colour or brush to another. Similarly, when working with these flowers, it is helpful to complete the placement of each variety in sequence so that the pattern of colour or texture of each one is strongly defined and balanced within the composition as a whole. A few stems can always be kept aside to provide last minute adjustment. Trying to work with several varieties at

the same time leads to confusion of the design function of each item.

Unlike painting, when it may be necessary to leave one area of colour to dry before working next to it, with dried flowers it is positively beneficial to work close to existing stems. It is much easier to handle the flowers and if the varieties are grouped close to one another, there is far less risk of damage to fragile stems. Large spaces can be left in between for the next flowers to be inserted.

Creating patterns

When designing the shapes of the flower groups in such a display it is important to remember the extent to which the eye is subconsciously aware of the pattern these shapes make. Lines or round blocks of colour – even of background filler material – will radically affect the overall composition by leading or stopping the eye's movement. Sometimes this effect may be intentional, but if the aim is to lead the eye through a design then an excellent shape to employ is an elongated teardrop. This is the shape so familiar in paisley-patterned fabric. With the flowers it produces a very natural flowing integration of shapes, which always looks good; the areas of colour have a visual impact but can trail off around or in between other varieties, allowing the eye to wander through the composition. This is similar to the way that plants mingle naturally while growing.

This technique of creating flowing groups of flowers is extremely helpful and has been used several times in the book. The most obvious example is the herbaceous border style fireplace on page 101.

Filling in the foreground

The next stage is to insert the fore- and middle-ground filler – the hydrangea heads. These bulky forms must not be dominant. If projecting out from the other flowers they will be top heavy and not perform their function of hiding the dry foam and lower stems. They can be set deep into the arrangement, providing background for the later focal flowers. However in the lower foreground they should project over the front rim of the container.

At this stage the arrangement still has a lot of empty spaces. Now is the time to use the lilac statice. This can be placed as individual stems at the perimeter of the display and concentrated as stronger masses of colour nearer the centre. Remaining gaps towards the centre then need to be filled with *Helichrysum*, wired together in clusters and tightly packed in among the other flowers for support. As with the other flowers, they create a balanced pattern of colour of their own. (*Helichrysum* colours are usually so strong that they can be set deep into an arrangement without risk of being hidden.)

Adding highlights and focal flowers

The addition of highlights comes next, with the touches of delicate, green *Alchemilla* and white *Anaphalis*. In this display, where the light comes from the side, these brighter colours have been accordingly concentrated on the left, and darker colours on the right to emphasize the three-dimensional form.

Finally, the peonies are carefully positioned, the ones at the focal centre of the display being viewed full-face and others from the side. In this design they need to stand slightly proud of the other flowers so that the light catches their dark petals.

Once a display is finished it can be enhanced by its strategic placement with other decorative items.

the future of dried flowers

Until now we have only considered the creation of designs that co-ordinate with their setting and existing fabrics. But there is the opportunity to create set piece still-life groups whereby a background – of paint or fabric – is specifically designed to enhance a dried flower design, thereby creating a complete work of art.

■ DRIED FLOWERS AS AN ART FORM

Van Gogh understood the character of sunflowers well when he painted them in a simple pottery jug; their form is so strong and their symbolism of sunny days so powerful that they need no accompaniment. In the design photographed here, the intention was to create a simple vase of sunflowers using the single, black-centred type rather than trying to reproduce Van Gogh's mixture of single and double yellow-flowered varieties.

An important growth characteristic of sunflowers is that they always turn to face the sun – the image that we have of them is therefore of seeing them full-face. It was important to reflect this in the way they were arranged. However, the big problem with dried sunflowers is that when they are hung upside-down to dry, the heads inevitably bend so that they are perpendicular to the stem rather than at an angle. When returned to the upright position, the heads therefore face upwards rather than forwards. To rectify this it was necessary to remove the heads with a diagonal cut and use a hot glue gun to re-fix them. The join was almost invisible and the effect looked entirely natural.

The chosen vase was wide from side to side, but narrowly elliptical in shape, thereby forcing the flowers to be arranged in a flat, front-facing design, a style that suited their character perfectly. The smooth clean lines of the pot contrasted with the crinkled texture of the petals and leaves, while the mottled surface suggested the shadows of dappled sunlight.

The piece of strongly streaked yellow and red fabric behind the display highlights the yellow of the petals and reinforces the image of strong summer sunlight. The rich ink blue of the background paint finish is the greatest possible

The bright background reinforces the image of hot summer created by the flowers.

contrast to the fabric – yellow-orange and orange-red being the split complementary colours opposite blue on the colour wheel.

The effect is dramatic in the extreme – like a piece of modern art – but took only a very short time to create. Sometimes it is the simplest ideas that turn out to be the most effective.

■ HARMONY IN BLUE

Here the scheme started with a glazed Chinese pot. A blue and white fabric with a leaf pattern similar to the vase was specifically chosen as background. The challenge was then to select flowers to complete the picture so that each element – the vase, the flowers and the fabric – all retained their integrity in equal harmony.

The rounded form of the vase suggested a dome-shaped design. There are not many dried flowers that are naturally blue, so the choice of varieties was limited. The blue of statice would have been too purple for this scheme. Larkspur could have offered lovely light blue or dark blue shades for a tall arrangement but its form would have been inappropriate in this compact design. *Echinops*, cornflower and lavender offered three tones of blue in different forms that complemented one another – grey-blue spheres, bright royal blue flowers and dark blue spires. The smooth grey leaves of *Eucalyptus* 'Silver Dollar' provided a splendid foil to the spiky *Echinops* and linked with the grey-blue shades in the fabric.

A white flower was needed to complete the scheme. *Achillea ptarmica* or *Anaphalis* would have

been too bright and carline thistles too big. The ideal choice was *Gypsophila* – a delicate and totally different flower form to the others. Its tiny flowers could give a visual lift to the collection without being too strong. The white element is dominant in both the vase and the fabric so it was important that the blue was the prominent colour among the flowers, otherwise the overall effect would have been distractingly busy.

The pot was packed with dry foam, the top projecting slightly above the edge so that the flowers around the rim could be inserted horizontally. Small groups of lavender were wired together, with their heads level, and distributed evenly in a dome shape, defining the height and width of the display. The *Echinops* were added next in groups of three or five, positioned close to the lavender. Sprigs of eucalyptus were interspersed through the arrangement, making sure that they did not project above the *Echinops.* Sprays of *Gypsophila* filled in the spaces. Finally, clusters of bright blue cornflowers were added, the weak stems being wired in groups of three or five. Their strong colour was a perfect match to the blue of the pot and the reason for adding them last was to ensure that they were not hidden by other flowers.

Against the wrong background all this careful styling would have been lost. But here the fabric has been hemmed to make a little wall-hanging and the background has been painted a soft grey-blue. The effect is calm, refined and stylish and worthy of being located where it can be admired in isolation. If only all dried flower arrangements could be displayed with such tender loving care!

PROJECT IDEAS AND INSPIRATION

You do not need to be a florist to be good at arranging dried flowers, you just need a genuine love of their colours and shapes and the confidence to be creative. Experience will teach you how to handle the flowers. It may be necessary to master new skills of wiring and the technique of using a glue gun and to learn some of the constructional methods needed for garlands or topiary trees but it is only through familiarity that you will understand which flowers are sturdy, which are fragile and which need to be wired for support. Only by observation and experimentation will you really learn how they react to light or humidity or how you can successfully combine colours.

The crucial thing is to play with shapes, styles and containers and not to be frightened of being adventurous. Mistakes are easy to disguise or rectify (and if you have grown and dried the flowers yourself there are no cost implications). A stem that has been cut too short can be artificially lengthened, a head that has been accidentally knocked off can be wired back into place, a variety that looks wrong can

be removed and replaced with another. Even if the work of a glue gun is near impossible to dislodge, any errors can at least be covered up! What cannot be disguised in any display is poor flowers. Be fussy about quality, have high standards and choose only the best.

Dried flower arrangements may vary from a simple bunch placed in a jug, to highly complex creations requiring planning, technical skills and a great deal of artistry. This book has already illustrated a range of design ideas to appeal to all tastes and abilities – to suit different rooms in the house, to be seasonal or to celebrate special occasions. Now, to round off, this chapter offers some guidelines to the many types of dried flower displays that can be created. But, whatever you make, and however proud you are of it, remember that it will not last for ever. Be ruthless. When it has faded and no longer looks its best, start again. There are always other flowers to use and new ideas to explore. Keep experimenting and above all, enjoy yourself!

seasonal projects

◼ VALENTINE WALL LATTICE

This is a simple but unusual project that uses just a small quantity of flowers. Here the images of hearts and red roses are combined with twiggy bows and red apples for a romantic Valentine's Day decoration that could remain on display all year round. The theme you choose does not need to be so specific but can use whatever flowers you have available plus any other decorative bits and pieces that seem appropriate. The method of construction is straightforward but the project can take time – especially deciding what to put where.

Creating a valentine lattice
The framework is made from the straight stems of willow bound together by raffia. Other straight stems such as hazel or dogwood would be equally suitable. Here the main sections are of three stems, and the inner gridwork of two or single stems, but you might need to adapt that to suit your design. It is important to make sure that there is a range of different-sized spaces and shapes which are well balanced as a composition. Lay the lattice flat on a tabletop while you work and when you are happy with the layout, tie the stems with raffia or twine.

Decide where the main focal elements are going to be and work from there, experimenting with placing items or flowers in different positions before finalizing the scheme. This design used hearts made from birch bark, bundles of red dogwood, paper apples, pottery leaves, little metal bells, bows of vine twigs, and painted feather butterflies. The flowers included sprays of roses, rose leaves and *Gypsophila,* as well as green and dyed burgundy honesty, sprigs of hops, and love-in-a mist pods combined with *Solidago.*

To secure the items in position, use reel wire or raffia and, if necessary, spots of glue. The flowers can be wired into little sprays and then bound to the main support wire, or threaded individually on to wires and glued into place. Make sure, when the support wires are attached to the framework, that they are pulled tight to prevent sagging. At this stage it is helpful to work on the lattice while it is hanging on the wall. The finished lattice can be supported directly by a couple of small nails in the wall or hung from a picture hook.

Other wall lattice ideas

Wall lattices can be made on any number of themes. Christmas is a good theme because there are lots of seasonal things to incorporate, such as fir cones, tree ornaments, gold poppies, bundles of cinnamon and ribbons. At Christmas time every surface at home seems to be crowded with cards, presents or candles so this could be a way of displaying Christmas decorations that does not take up shelf or floor space. It would also make a lovely welcoming display in a hallway. For a kitchen wall lattice, food items could be used – strings of dried apples and oranges, small pomegranates, corks, spices like star anise, little wooden measuring spoons, pastry cutters and sprigs of herbs. Lattices can also be personalized, for example, for a child's bedroom, with little toys or carved animals, or for a relative, incorporating favourite flowers, special fabrics and perhaps a quotation or photograph.

*With summer hats you
are at liberty to be as
extravagant and flamboyant
as you like.*

AUTUMNAL WHEATSHEAVES

Wheatsheaves and stooks are simple but effective decorations that suit many locations as permanent or festive features. In the home they look good in the kitchen or they make useful slim-line wall decorations in narrow hallways or stairwells. Their neutral colouring blends with most colour schemes but they can be enlivened with the addition of coloured ties or sprays of flowers. For summer or autumn weddings, they are excellent for decorating marquee poles, chair backs, barns, halls, church doors and pew ends.

Free-standing stook

To make a simple free-standing stook, as featured in the harvest festival display on page 109, you will need eight bunches of wheat. Remove the rubber bands and shake the individual bunches upside-down on a tabletop until all the heads are level.

SUMMER HAT

A hat decorated with dried flowers is a charming fashion accessory for a sunny summer wedding but check the weather forecast before you wear it – a shower of rain would not improve its looks. Straw hats are ideal subjects for adornment and can be graced with anything from a single peony or a spray of wheat stems and cornflowers to a mass of blooms that is, literally, full to the brim.

A glue gun is essential. Start by wiring together individual sprays of the smaller flowers – larkspur, *Achillea ptarmica* and *Gypsophila* – and dividing up the hydrangeas into smaller florets. Decide whether the main concentration of flowers will be at the front or back, or asymmetrically placed at the side. First glue the larkspur into position ensuring that the stems are consistently angled, perhaps spiralling around the brim or radiating out

from a flower group. Add the *Achillea*, some of the hydrangea florets and then carefully position the large peonies, making sure that all the stems are covered. In-fill with *Gypsophila* and the remaining hydrangeas and finally glue on the rose heads.

The hat illustrated used 'Sarah Bernhardt' peonies, 'Jaguar' roses and the smaller side-shoots of pink larkspur. The soft *Anaphalis margaritacea* would have been an alternative to the *Achillea*. Instead of ribbon, maize leaves were dampened and gently moulded to form bows and the 'tails' trimmed to shape. These obviously need to be planned into the design at an early stage.

After the wedding, the hat can be hung on the wall as a permanent decoration and memento.

*A free-standing stook
of green wheat.*

A small flat-backed wall sheaf designed as pew-end decoration for a wedding.

Lay all eight bunches level together over a piece of string and tie them (not too tightly) around the middle. The next stage is easiest done sitting down with the stook laid across your lap. Twist the whole bundle so that the stems spiral and then gradually start shaping the stook using the flat of the hand to push the heads into place. Keep turning the stook over as you do this and gradually tighten the string. Slowly the stook will begin to take shape and, when you are satisfied with its appearance, tie the string as tight as you can and cover it with plaited twine or raffia.

To trim the base of the stems, lay the stook on a table so that the ends of the stems over-hang the edge. With the centre line of the stook at right angles to the table edge, keep turning the stook over and trimming just the longest stems with secateurs until they are level.

Free-standing stooks can also be made using the wiring method demonstrated in the bridesmaid's posy (see page 143). Stooks and sheaves can be made of wheat, oats or *Triticale*. (Barley is not so suitable because of the brittleness of the awns.) For long-term decoration natural green rather than golden or dyed grasses are probably best, even though they will fade eventually.

Flat-backed wheatsheaf

The flat-backed sheaf illustrated was made as a pew-end decoration for a wedding, using two bunches of green wheat plus a few stems of white larkspur, poppies and lavender.

To make a sheaf like this, split each of the bunches of wheat into two halves (each containing about 30–40 stems). Strip off the leaves and gently tap each of the four smaller bunches upside-down on a tabletop to make all the heads level. Place a piece of twine horizontally on the table (ready to tie the sheaf later), and lay one of the bunches vertically across it; this will form the centre back of the sheaf. Place the second bunch at a 45° angle to the centre bunch, crossing the first one halfway down, to form one side. Place the third bunch similarly to form the other side. Place the fourth bunch centrally to form the lower front of the sheaf.

Tie with the twine (not too tightly yet) and gently adjust the position of heads, individually pulling them up or pushing them down until an even shape is achieved. Keep checking the back of the sheaf and pulling up any heads that are hidden from view. (When making further sheaves, try adjusting the shape of the bunches before they are laid down, so making this later stage easier.) If flowers are to be added they can be gently inserted into the sheaf now, or incorporated at the earlier stage.

Once everything is in place, tie the twine tightly and cover with a raffia bow, ribbon or plaited twine. Trim the ends of the stems into a slight arc shape. The height of the sheaf is a matter of personal preference – if cut too short it can look top heavy but it invariably looks well balanced if the tie is in the middle.

A larger sheaf can be made using four bunches of wheat. The method for making is identical but the bunches are used whole not split in half.

*This Christmas table
decoration will last
throughout the
festive season.*

*Winter door rings can be an
adventurous collection of
dried fruits and spices mixed
with seed heads.*

CHRISTMAS TABLE CENTRE

Table centres of dried flowers are especially popular at Christmas when the entertaining season can last for several weeks and there is little spare time for arranging fresh flowers. Most festive table decorations would incorporate candles, but *only* do this with dried flowers if the arrangement is given a precautionary spray with a fire retardant and the candles are *never* left unsupervised.

Apart from flowers in traditional colourings of red, green and gold, Christmas arrangements can also be made in silver and icy blue, or burgundy. Red roses and gold poppies are forever popular and dried fruit and spices always look appropriate, but a splendid focal flower to use is the carline thistle. It links to silver and gold with its shiny outer petals and creamy coloured centre and is dramatic, unusual and eyecatching.

To be practical, table centre designs need to be low in height, so as not to prevent guests talking to one another across the table, and to be relatively compact so that they do not take up the space needed for crockery and cutlery. The shallow plastic trays used by florists for fresh flowers are equally appropriate for dried flowers and simply need a block of dry foam to be taped into place.

Creating a table centre
The Christmas table centre illustrated was made in a 50cm (20in) long plastic tray using two blocks of dry foam. The chosen flowers were white larkspur (the shorter side shoots rather than the big leader stems), glycerined green beech leaves, golden rod,

WINTER DOOR RING

Fresh wreaths for the front door last for only a few weeks and are specifically associated with Christmas, but here is an idea for a wreath of dried flowers that could last throughout the winter season. It cannot unfortunately be recommended for an outside door but is ideal in a porch or for a front door to a flat in an apartment block. It can, of course, also be used on an internal door or wall – or, if decorated on both sides, at a window. (The colourings of this design have a grey rather than green background so should last adequately well for a season when the sun is not strong and daylight hours are limited.)

A flat woven basketware ring is best for this design, but a circular base of dry foam could also be used. The plant material used was *Eucalyptus* 'Silver Dollar', *Anaphalis*, 'Dumosa', gold-sprayed poppies, and Chinese lanterns, with dried orange slices, mandarins, bundles of cassia sticks and a

silvery grey-blue netting ribbon. These colours show well against dark painted or wooden backgrounds but alternative more strongly coloured varieties could be used that would work with white or any light paintwork.

Begin by threading the lanterns, cassia and orange slices on to raffia and tying them on to the bottom section of the ring. Then, starting at the top and working down each side symmetrically, glue into position sprigs of eucalyptus, *Anaphalis* and individual poppy heads, overlapping the varieties so that the stems are covered. (You may find it easiest to work with the ring on a table with the strings trailing over the edge.)

Tie the ribbon into a double bow and fix it at the top, placing a mandarin or bundle of cassia at its centre. Use small sprigs of 'Dumosa' to fill in any gaps in the design, particularly around the perimeter. Finally, glue into place a few cassia bundles, orange slices and some bright clusters of Chinese lanterns.

golden yarrow, love-in-a-mist, gold poppies, red roses and carline thistles. To recreate this yourself insert individual stems of the larkspur first, starting from table level so as to conceal the container and radiating out from the ends of the tray. Arrange the larkspur in a zigzag line across the top of the arrangement to the middle of the other side and then back again. Then place the love-in-a mist in groups of about five stems, following the line of the larkspur. Use the golden rod and yarrow to in-fill the areas on either side and add the beech leaves at table level to cover the foam and tray. Place the carline thistles strategically with a central group of five following the diagonal line of the larkspur, balanced by a couple of other heads at either end. Use groups of gold poppies to give a festive sparkle and then reinforce the design with red roses (some in groups, some singly), weaving through the zigzag line from one end to the other. To give a finishing touch of contrasting texture add a few loops of Christmas ribbon.

If being made commercially, the groups of flowers would need to be wired together for insertion into the foam to ensure they were not dislodged while in transit or on display, but for domestic purposes wiring would only be necessary if the block was not large enough to take the number of stems, or if the stems of the flowers were particularly brittle.

Children enjoy helping to create unusual Christmas decorations, but do not let them use a glue gun.

■ AN ALTERNATIVE CHRISTMAS TREE

Traditional fir trees can take up a lot of space and when the needles drop it can be quite a problem. For something different, try using wintry stems as a basis on which to hang your decorations.

Here stems of red dogwood have been fixed into foam in a metal vase. A mound of *Anaphalis* creates the image of snow. Gold poppy heads and Chinese lanterns have been glued to the ends of the branches and bundles of gold-sprayed vine twigs hung alongside the wooden decorations.

wedding flowers

So much thought goes into the preparation for a wedding day: making bookings, organizing catering, buying a dress, decorating the cake. Some things can be organized in advance but many jobs cannot be done until the last minute and one of those is the arrangement of the fresh flowers – the bouquet, the bridesmaids' head-dresses, the buttonholes and corsages, the table centre arrangements and the decoration of the church and reception area. The use of dried flowers is well worth considering for many reasons.

BENEFITS FOR THE BRIDE OF USING DRIED FLOWERS

There is, understandably, an increasing trend towards the use of dried flowers for at least some, if not all, of the floral decorations for weddings. First and foremost, from a bride's point of view, the use of dried flowers is going to ensure a lasting memento of her wedding day. Most brides are sad to see their all-important bouquet wither and wilt and ultimately have to be discarded. Some seek to have a fresh bouquet preserved by drying or pressing, but the process is not always successful because of the varieties used and results can be disappointing.

Because dried flowers are available throughout the year, the choice is not restricted to seasonal varieties (or costly out-of-season imports). Also the range of flowers available allows co-ordination with any colour scheme. The bride can decide what she wants well in advance and see the articles made up and finished for approval before the big

day, so avoiding last minute problems. Advance or post-event photographic sessions are also possible; these are sometimes needed if a wedding is planned to take place abroad in an exotic location. And on the subject of weddings away from home, a bride can take her bouquet with her rather than having to rely on an unknown florist at her destination. (Bouquets being taken abroad should omit poppies and cereal or grass varieties as these can be subject to import restrictions in other countries.)

With strict financial budgets these days, the longer a floral display lasts, the better value it is perceived to be. The brief, albeit appreciative, attention which fresh wedding flowers receive can seem an extravagance when longer lasting alternatives are available. Not only the bridal bouquet, but all the corsages, bridesmaids' posies and circlets can be kept afterwards if made of dried or preserved flowers. Garlands from the church or the reception table can be used to decorate the home, and the table centres or pew-end displays given as presents to friends, relatives or helpers.

Some brides may see the use of dried flowers not only as a way of keeping costs down but also of giving the pleasure of personal family involvement in the preparations. A flower arranger in the family can make up decorations such as table centres, buttonholes, and so on in advance, thus spreading the cost and the workload over a period of time. Professional florists need not fear that their own skills are being undermined – their expertise is invaluable in the more complicated bouquets and garlands which many people would find intimidating to make.

ADVANTAGES FOR A FLORIST

The pressure on a florist, working with fresh flowers to a tight deadline and to very specific instructions, can be great – and the situation is not helped by a client's anxiety that everything should be perfect. The removal of the problem of limited time must be one of the main advantages of working with dried flowers for a wedding. All the displays can be made up for approval in advance and the florist can be assured of the quality and availability of all the flowers before starting work.

Samples can be kept in stock to help prospective brides make their selections. Samples are so much better than photographs to give inspiration, show colours and allow the bride to see and feel different shapes and styles of bouquet in her hand.

Larger, more expensive displays such as topiary trees, pedestal arrangements or elaborate garlands can be made available for hire, though obviously adequate storage space is needed where the flowers will not be damaged by light, humidity, moths or mice.

CHOOSING WEDDING FLOWERS

Choosing flowers for her wedding may be the first time that a young woman has had to seriously consider which flower varieties she likes and which design styles appeal to her. In addition, there are the complexities of colour co-ordinating the flowers to dress fabrics. Sometimes the choice is made easier by certain flowers having particular associations, for instance, marjoram (*Origanum vulgare*) was used by the Ancient Greeks in wedding crowns, *Gypsophila* symbolizes fidelity and purity, and the Latin name of golden rod, *Solidago*, means to join together or make whole. Love-in-a-mist (*Nigella damascena*) is an obvious choice for the bride, just as cornflower is a must for the groom's buttonhole – traditionally, a young man would put cornflowers in his pocket as a symbol of being in love. At country weddings, wheat and poppies were always considered to be symbols of fertility.

As focal flowers, peonies are excellent. 'Sarah Bernhardt' is a very soft light pink and shows up well against purple marjoram, but the cream 'Duchesse de Nemours' and dark pink 'Monsieur Jules Elie' are also useful, if not so readily available.

Roses are essential as romantic symbols of love. The white 'Tineke' dries with a lovely greenish tinge, 'Gerdo' has a useful peach colouring, 'Kiss' is a delicate light pink, and 'Europa' is an excellent dark pink that holds its colour reasonably well. 'Mercedes' is the best bright red. 'Jaguar', when dried, is probably too dark a red for wedding work and unlikely to photograph well from a distance.

The whitest dried flowers are probably the white statice *Limonium sinuatum* and the Australian Ixodia daisy. Slightly creamier whites are found with *Achillea ptarmica*, larkspur, *Gypsophila*, *Anaphalis* and 'Dumosa'. Then there is the cream *Helichrysum* which is a buttermilk colour that can be tinged pink or yellow.

Hydrangeas and eucalyptus are excellent background fillers. Of the grasses, wheat and oats are very appropriate for summer or autumn

weddings and canary grass has neat, compact heads ideal for bouquets, posies and garlands. The small grasses like *Setaria viridus* and quaking grass are suitable for delicate corsages, whereas the larger Italian millet, sorghum and maize tops are valuable in big pedestal displays.

Green hop bines are unbeatable as value-for-money garlands for churches, halls and marquees, but because of restricted availability are really only suitable for late summer or autumn weddings – unless acquired well in advance.

The examples in this chapter illustrate two colour schemes suitable for seasonal weddings – a spring combination of blues and yellows for bridesmaids and a summer bouquet of pinks.

▪ THE BRIDE'S BOUQUET

The most important floral piece at a wedding is always the bride's bouquet – it features in most of the photographs so needs to look good from a distance and, laid next to the wedding cake at the reception, may be closely inspected by the guests. It must complement the colour and design theme of the dress, be comfortable to hold, and withstand several hours of handling. However, being an item that the bride will want to keep, a dried flower bouquet is unlikely to have to withstand being tossed to one of the bridesmaids!

Remember that its design must ensure that the varieties used are not too fragile and that its shape is relatively compact since long, trailing elements are likely to be damaged. Delicate, pale colours will fade more quickly so, if the long-term look of the

bouquet matters, be sure to include some stronger colours for background contrast. Dyed flowers should be avoided unless it is absolutely certain that the colours will not stain the dress.

Hand-tied posies are a neat, compact shape but also popular are the more informal flat-backed bouquets that can be held over one arm. For the latter, panicum millet is a good variety to include as it drapes and hangs beautifully. Both styles of bouquet can maximize the use of trailing ties of ribbon or raffia. Other more complex shapes are best built around the purpose-made posy holders which consist of a piece of rectangular or dome-shaped dry foam contained by a plastic framework with a moulded handle.

Creating a bouquet

A circular posy holder was used as the basis for the bouquet illustrated here. An S-shape was designed to give a sense of movement and a range of flowers chosen to be representative of a summer garden – white larkspur, light pink 'Sarah Bernhardt' peonies, bright pink 'Kiss' roses, purple marjoram, *Gypsophila, Achillea ptarmica*, lilac statice, pink poker statice, love-in-a-mist and *Alchemilla mollis*.

Insert the white larkspur first to establish the shape and direction of the bouquet. Then build up the centre block of flowers, starting with the marjoram and setting it low down in the foam in an S- shape to provide background contrast to the paler focal flowers being added later. Place the large peonies next, having softened and teased open their petals by gently steaming them over a

kettle. Bearing in mind where the roses are planned to be, fill in the sides of the bouquet with lilac statice (a delightful colour contrast to the peonies), *Achillea* and love-in-a-mist. Place each variety so as to strengthen the sense of movement in the design, following the teardrop or 'paisley' pattern shape mentioned in the last chapter. The flowers chosen for the centre of the bouquet are round in form and densely packed together to be viewed full-face whereas the flowers radiating out on either side are of long thin form and more loosely arranged, being viewed from the side.

Use the long wavy line of the poker statice to link the pink centre of the bouquet to the linear form of the white larkspur, and the maize leaves (carefully chosen for their individual shapes) as background to soften the straightness of the larkspur. Use the lower side-shoots of the larkspur, still in green bud, in small groups to blend the bold full-flowered stems in towards the more delicate centre of the bouquet. Add *Alchemilla* at the sides as a filler to give a freshness to the colour scheme.

Place the roses (having been carefully steamed open a little, like the peonies) slightly proud of the background flowers, to ensure that their colour and sinuous pattern are prominent. Placing them late in the sequence like this ensures that they are not damaged while other flowers are being inserted. For a finishing touch, sprinkle a few sprigs of *Gypsophila*, throughout the design.

All the flowers used need to be wired for insertion into the foam. The surface area of foam in these posy holders is small and it is not possible to insert this number of stems directly.

Handling and aftercare

Care needs to be taken when handling this bouquet to ensure that the delicate tips of the larkspur are not damaged. Glue could be used to give stems extra security. A light spray of fixer can help prevent any petal drop. As a long-term memento, the bouquet is best kept away from direct light. An anti-static spray will help reduce dust and the hiding of a mothball among the flowers will deter insect damage.

The groom, ushers and special
guests can all be given sprays
of flowers that link with the
bride's bouquet.

Circlets and hand-tied posies
for the bridesmaids can be
made well in advance.

CORSAGES AND BUTTONHOLES

Far more interesting than the traditional carnation, small sprays of dried flowers are very eyecatching and can be personalized to suit fashion colourings. Because they are unusual you will find that they often draw comments… and they should suffer no more crushing from fond embraces than would a fresh flower!

Sturdy, small-scale flowers that will not readily drop petals or shed seeds are needed. In the illustration, the groom's buttonhole is made of *Setaria viridis*, lavender, *Alchemilla mollis* and *Gypsophila* with a central dark pink 'Europa' rosebud. Wire the stems together for stability and then tie with raffia – a spot of glue under the rose and at the back of the stems adds extra security.

NATURAL CONFETTI

Petals of dried roses, peonies and larkspur, as well as lavender, *Achillea ptarmica* and small *Helichrysum* buds make charming natural confetti. So when you are working at the table be sure to keep all the dropped petals and any left over buds from a display and put them to good use!

BRIDESMAIDS' CIRCLETS

The simplest form of head adornment is a small spray of flowers glued to a comb or hair slide, but a more elaborate tiara for the bride and a circlet for the bridesmaid are delightful. Full crowns of flowers have a rustic charm, especially on children, and look appropriate for bridesmaids carrying small baskets of dried flowers or petals that they can strew as confetti.

The circlets illustrated here have a spring colour scheme of blue and yellow, one of them using 'Golden Time' roses, hydrangeas, *Achillea ptarmica*, *Nigella*, *Gypsophila* and cornflowers, and the other using the roses, cornflower and *Gypsophila* but with *Anaphalis* and wheat.

Making a circlet
First measure the head size and make a ring (slightly larger in circumference) of 90 gauge wire; bind this with florists' tape. Make up small sprays of each of the flower varieties, individually binding them with fine reel wire. Place one or two sprays of different flowers into position, with the stems pointing around the ring, and tightly bind them with tape. Add further sprays, ensuring that each covers the stems of the previous ones and ensuring that all tape is concealed.

When the circle is complete, the final spray can be secured to the stems of the first with fine reel wire. Rose heads can be quite brittle to work with, so if any break off during the taping or seem insecure they can be fixed more firmly with the aid of a hot glue gun.

■ HAND-TIED POSIES

In earlier times, when standards of general hygiene were not as good, nosegays of strongly scented flowers and herbs were carried to ward off smells and keep germs at bay. Nowadays hand-tied posies are a popular form of floral design, pretty enough for a bride or bridesmaids to carry or to offer as excellent hostess gifts or Mother's Day presents. Made of scented herbs and lavender, they are also ideal for taking on hospital visits because the patient can keep them and take them home afterwards. Colour co-ordinated to fabrics, hand-tied bouquets can also be a decorative element in the home – either free-standing or laid casually on their side, as in the photograph of a bridesmaid's posy. In this posy blue hydrangea florets were used for the centre, surrounded by carefully spaced roses and cornflowers, with more hydrangeas; the outer rings consisted of *Achillea ptarmica*, love-in-a-mist, marjoram and *Gypsophila*.

Making a successful hand-tied posy requires careful preparation and manual dexterity. The posies are built from concentric rings of different flowers and their visual success depends on the combination of textures and colours. Because this type of posy displays flowers full-face, it is best to use compact varieties of a rounded form. The long thin flower spikes of larkspur and *Amaranthus* are not ideal, but peonies, roses, lavender, poppies, marjoram, *Carthamus, Helichrysum*, sage, *Achillea, Alchemilla, Gypsophila, Nigella,* cornflower, linseed, *Echinops*, statice and, canary grass, all work very well in posies.

Making a hand-tied posy

First, trim excessively long stems, remove leaves and disentangle clusters of flowers. It is worth taking time now to arrange the flowers neatly on the workbench because while the bouquet is being made it needs to be held in one hand, leaving only a single hand free to prepare and tie in the other flowers. The centre of the design can be a large single flower, like a peony or a cluster of smaller flowers like *Helichrysum*. Take a reel of fine wire and secure it tightly around the central stem or stems, about 50–75mm (2–3in) from the top. Choose the flowers for the next ring and, taking groups of a few stems, make sure the heads are level and bind each group to the centre working with a continuous length of reel wire. At this stage, keep the stems vertical. Make sure the central flower is not hidden; the aim is to produce a slightly domed shape that displays the character of all the varieties.

Once the central two or three rings are in place, it is time to start angling the stems so that they splay out to form a spiral. With the next ring, place each cluster of flowers at an angle across the posy and bind it into place as before. Continue until the posy is the desired size, finishing with a 'collar' or frill of something like hydrangea, *Gypsophila, Alchemilla* or perhaps *Carthamus*. Wind the wire around several times and tie off tightly.

Cut the stems level at the base to make sure the posy will stand upright; it is sometimes helpful to cut the central stems shorter so that the outer stems provide the support. A shorter posy is more stable and may look better than a tall one. The bouquet can be finished with bows of ribbon, raffia or twine.

special occasions and gifts

BOUQUET D'HIVER AND GIFT BOUQUETS

As mentioned in Chapter 1, in the time before commercial glasshouse production when fresh flowers were only available locally in season, garden flowers were specially grown for drying to decorate houses in the winter months. These were known as 'bouquets d'hiver' - or winter bouquets.

The traditional and easily made flat-backed bouquets are always well received as gifts. They can be hung up for display just as they are, laid flat on a surface such as on a hall table or chest of drawers, put straight into a vase or taken apart and rearranged to another design.

The potential choice of flowers is endless; these bouquets need a range of long and rounded flower forms which will complement one another in shape, texture and colour. Grasses, maize tops, green honesty, eucalyptus or preserved leaves are useful background elements to establish the bouquet's length and width. Tall spires of larkspur can be added next for summer colour, or *Amaranthus paniculatus* and Chinese lanterns for an autumnal look. *Carthamus, Nigella, Achillea millefolium* and marjoram are useful fillers to contrast in colour with the main flowers. Lavender, sage, oregano and thyme can be included for their

The small amount of extra time and effort needed to personalise gifts is always rewarded by warm appreciation.

scent. *Anaphalis, Achillea ptarmica, Gypsophila* and 'Dumosa' give highlights if required. *Helichrysum* is excellent as the main focal variety in simple designs but also useful as a colour link to offset flowers like roses or peonies in more glamorous upmarket bouquets.

Making a bouquet d'hiver

The bouquet d'hiver illustrated was made in a subtle colour scheme of cool wintery blue and white that looked forward to spring with some lemon, pale green and a touch of pink for warmth. The design used green honesty, lavender, larkspur, love-in-a-mist, *Anaphalis, Helichrysum* and also 'Kiss' roses.

Build up the bouquet starting from the back, working with it either laid flat on a workbench or, preferably, held continually in one hand. It is a good idea to prepare all the flowers beforehand so that they can be picked up and simply laid in place. For a bouquet of this size the flowers do not need to be wired in groups. Place the varieties so as to lead the eye down towards the main concentration of flowers, in the lower section of the bouquet, above the tie. Balance the groups of flowers in colour and size, rather than placing them symmetrically, so that they flow through and around one another. When complete, tie the stems tightly with wire or twine, then cover this with an ornamental tie of raffia or ribbon.

Very large bouquets with weighty elements – such as the design for the dining room wall illustrated on page 102 which includes thick stems of beech and large artichokes – need wiring

progressively as the design is built up, to secure the stems in position. In that instance, the stems of *Atriplex* and Italian millet happened to be too short to stretch the full length of the bouquet and so were attached to the beech branches behind with strong reel wire. The *Carthamus* and poppies were likewise secured back and the heavy artichokes tied into place to prevent them moving position when the bouquet was hung on the wall. Heavy bouquets like this need to be made while laid flat on a workbench.

GIFT WRAPPING

A gift can be made very special and personal by a little extra care in its presentation – and it is always greatly appreciated. Decorations can be seasonal (mini pumpkins or apple slices in the autumn), romantic (roses and lavender are unbeatable), have a personal association (a favourite flower) or be on the theme of the parcel's contents (herbs and spices for a culinary gift). Christmas offers many opportunities for gold poppies, bundles of cinnamon, dried orange slices, pomegranates or strings of green bay leaves, and each present can be decorated differently. The items can be wired together and tied on with raffia or glued direct on to the paper. Fruit slices and bay leaves can be threaded on to strings using a darning needle.

The wrapping paper for the presents in the illustration continues the dried flower theme. There are many attractive handmade papers available now which include leaves of grasses and flower petals such as marigolds and *Bougainvillea.*

CELEBRATION SWAGS AND GARLANDS

Swags and garlands are glorious for special occasions and are well worth the time and effort it takes to make them because they can be enjoyed for many months after the event. Technically, a swag hangs vertically whereas a garland drapes horizontally, although the two are often combined. Both can be made purely by wiring methods, ensuring that each group of flowers overlaps the previous one (see the description of the garlands on the corkscrew willow branch on page 119). Where a greater volume of flowers is required, a pliable base of moss encased in chicken wire is made and the flowers are wired into position. Alternatively, dry foam can be used, either secured in place by chicken wire or held in pre-formed plastic cages that join together in sections. A fabric backing can be added if necessary to prevent the wire scratching the surface behind.

It can be fun to incorporate fabric into swags. Not only does it give a rich and sumptuous effect but it also reduces the quantity of flowers needed.

Creating a celebration swag
This celebration piece for a golden wedding anniversary used a fine white organza printed with gold swirls. For this project, several blocks of foam need to be halved in depth, cut to size and then bound by chicken wire. A gold-sprayed netting of woven vine twigs is secured in place and the fabric pinned in position with wires. (Thick material will hold its own shape but fine fabrics can be given extra bulk with crumpled tissue paper.) The material should ultimately look as if it is flowing through the design, weaving in and out of the flowers and leading the eye from one part of the design to the other. Patterned fabrics need to be offset by a simple collection of well-chosen varieties whereas plainer fabrics can enhance a more complex pattern of flowers.

In this instance, the colour scheme is restricted to cream, gold and green. 'Duchesse de Nemours' peonies, carline thistles, larkspur and *Gypsophila*, are set against bright green *Amaranthus paniculatus*. A festive air is added by gold poppies, pine cones and a few clusters of gilded artificial fruit.

The two focal points are first identified by groups of peonies. Insert the green *Amaranthus* and white larkspur, lining them up with the peonies and radiating them out to give a strong direction to the design. Build up the design by adding the gilded fruit, then the poppies in larger clusters, flowing out from the focal points. Insert single heads of carline thistles deep into the other flowers and in-fill the remaining spaces with delicate drifts of *Gypsophila* and wired fir cones.

An identical constructional method can be used for an arc of flowers to grace a doorway or alcove.

Foam cut to shape and then bound with chicken wire provides a good base on which to build up a display.

designs for the home

Hopefully the illustrations throughout this book will have given some inspiration for projects for different rooms in the house and on the following pages are a few other specific home designs to try. They can all be adapted to suit the colour schemes of individual rooms.

Remember always to keep any petals that fall off and any broken flowers or oddments left over to make into pot-pourri. Think about scents, colours and shapes when blending mixes together and feel free to include other unusual ingredients to add character, such as exotic seed-pods or cones sprayed gold, strips of dried orange peel, shells, leaves cut into star shapes, and so on. The leaves of mint, lemon verbena and lemon balm give a fresh scent, some rose petals have a strong perfume and the smell of hops is traditionally considered to be a cure for insomnia. For other more powerful aromas purchase one of the specially prepared pot-pourri oils that are available.

Swags and garlands can be linked to their surroundings by the inclusion of off-cut pieces of the room's furnishing fabric.

*This simple method of
constructing a ring can be
applied to a range of flowers.*

*The complete herb ring –
ideal for a kitchen wall.*

▪ HERB RING

The principle of making one of these delightful
herb rings applies also to other flower themes
where a wide ring base is being used. These
wreaths look wonderful in a kitchen decorated
with herbs and spices, but can have a more
autumnal theme and colouring for harvest festival
or Thanksgiving with wheat, dried fruit, mini
pumpkins and maize cobs, seed-heads and
Chinese lanterns. Alternatively they can be made
of individual species, such as lavender or wheat, to
create a dramatic impact from the use of a single
colour or texture.

All that is needed is twine and possibly reel wire.
This example used hops for their wonderful fresh
green colour, marjoram for its contrasting colour of
deep purple, lavender for its scent, poppies for
their bold shape, grey sage for its texture, tansy for
its sparkle of gold and *Alchemilla* as a delicate filler
especially on the perimeter. A wreath like this can
be hung direct on to a nail or picture hook in the
wall. Alternatively, make a loop of thick wire
covered with tape and attach it to the back before
you begin working with the flowers.

To make a herb ring

Start by preparing all the material, disentangling
flowers and trimming the stems to the correct
length. Wiring is not essential but for ease of
assembly some of the marjoram and lavender can
be wired in small sprays. Tie the string securely to
the framework and lay one or two sprays in
position, so that the stems radiate outwards,

following the line of the wreath. Wind the string
around once or twice to hold the stems in place,
then add another spray of a different variety so
that it covers the stems of the ones before; repeat
until the ring is complete. Every so often, knot the
string securely to the wreath before continuing. It

does not matter whether you work clockwise or
anti-clockwise, so long as the stems radiate
outwards in a consistent pattern. Make sure that
the circle is even, around the perimeter and on the
inside of the ring. Occasional slices of apple can be
wired into place at the end.

A long-lasting and extremely eye-catching kitchen display that could also be hung from a high ceiling.

■ HANGING BASKET

The wire framework made for outdoor hanging baskets can be used equally successfully for dried flowers in the home. The baskets can be hung from beams, in alcoves or suspended from hooks in the ceiling – stairwells are an appropriate location.

One design style is to replicate the image of the planted basket by lining the base with flat moss (instead of fresh moss), filling it with dry foam (instead of soil) and then 'planting' it with a cascading collection of varieties. (panicum millet, hydrangeas and wired clusters of *Helichrysum* are ideal for this.) This style is useful where the basket is hung just above eye-level so that the moss and the flowers are both visible.

The other style especially suitable for high locations concentrates all the flowers around the underside. It can either be shaped like a round ball or designed to trail down. To decorate marquees or party rooms, the balls can be made of coloured 'Dumosa' or delicate *Gypsophila* interspersed with peonies. For something more dramatic, try creating a glowing sun of double yellow sunflowers. The trailing style can be emphasized by using *Amaranthus caudatus,* larkspur and Italian millet. If being viewed from below, the top of the basket, can be filled with 'Dumosa'.

Creating a hanging basket display
The illustration shows a hanging basket for a kitchen. The 'ingredients' are all on a culinary theme – chillies, pumpkins, hops, marjoram, millet, artichokes, wheat, poppies, cinnamon, fruit slices,

A veritable forest of topiary trees reminiscent of a bonsai design.

onions heads and fungi. The design combines the two styles already described, using moss but incorporating a trailing effect.

First line the basket with flat moss and fill it with dry foam (two or three blocks are usually enough). Allow the foam to project above the side of the basket so that the flowers can be made to 'trail' more easily. Starting at the top, 'plant' first the groups of wheat, then poppies, marjoram and millet – having first trimmed them and bound them with stub wires to make insertion easier. Place each group close to its neighbour to leave plenty of room for subsequent varieties, rather than dotting the groups around and then having small awkward spaces to fill. Fill the remaining spaces with single artichokes and onion heads and groups of fungi, securing the latter by wires or glue. Bind the chillies, orange slices and pumpkins together in trails using reel wire and tie them to the basket or fix them into the foam with stub wires. Add the cinnamon and then lastly, arrange the fragile hops so that they casually trail down through the arrangement for a more informal finish.

■ TOPIARY TREES

Topiary trees may appear complicated to make and be off-putting to a beginner. The challenge is to make the base and stem secure and stable. Once that has been achieved the rest is comparatively easy and the possibilities are endless.

Because topiary designs are invariably taller than they are wide they can overbalance unless the base is sufficiently weighty. For this reason pots are better containers than baskets, but even they need to be of a suitable size so that the tree does not look top heavy. The 'trunks' of the trees can be made from short pieces of branch or, for more unusual designs, sections of contorted willow or hazel. An alternative is to tie together several thinner twigs or sticks of cassia. Dry foam in the pots is not usually strong enough to hold anything other than miniature trees. It is therefore advisable to secure the trunks in either a hard drying plasticine or plaster of Paris. The trunk of a very large topiary tree may need to be secured with a large metal screw through the hole at the base of the pot.

The top part of the tree can be constructed from either moss or cones and balls of dry-foam. Large pre-shaped foam can be expensive to buy and it may be cheaper to glue the standard blocks together and cut them to shape as necessary. For assymetrical or 'cloud-shaped' flower masses, ordinary fresh moss that has been allowed to dry can be encased in chicken wire, moulded into shape and secured firmly with wire and staples to the trunk. These constructions then allow for a variety of different effects to be developed, such as tightly packed masses of *Echinops* or poppies, lavender dotted with rosebuds, balls of glued leaves or star anise, or informal collections of small flowers like *Anaphalis, Eryngium* and *Lonas*. It is usually necessary to wire the flowers in groups so that the stems do not take up too much space in the foam. Fine-stemmed varieties like lavender are certainly easier to handle in clumps.

*The flowers need to be
wired in clusters to make
the floral sheaf.*

*Rustic in character but sophisticated
in design, this sheaf looks impressive
over a living room mantelpiece.*

Creating a topiary forest

For the rather zany forest of topiary trees in the photograph on the previous page, a heavy, shallow, glazed pottery dish was used with branches of corkscrew willow that had been sharpened at the top end. Cones of dry foam were covered in flat moss using a glue gun and then spiked on to the branches and glued into place. The base was also covered in flat moss, with a few fungi 'growing' at one side for natural effect.

Creating these 'trees' was a simple and quick process. What took time in this design was selecting the right shaped branches to blend with one another and achieving a balance in the size, height and distribution of the 'trees'. Less elaborate designs with individual mossed trees look good in simple glazed or antiqued gold pots. They can also be made into miniature Christmas trees, decorated with small gold baubles, and used as matching pairs to adorn a mantelpiece or chest of drawers.

▪ FLORAL WALL SHEAF

The principles underlying the making of this impressive sheaf shown opposite, can be applied to other wall decorations of different size or character. They could be made of just wheat or lavender, or be a different shape – maybe a circle of yellows to represent a flaming sun.

These flowers were chosen on an autumnal theme, concentrating on yellows, oranges and greens, but with blue as the important comple-mentary colour. The actual varieties used were

sunflowers, giant knapweed (*Centaurea macro-cephala*), orange *Carthamus* and *Helichrysum*, *Echinops*, *Nigella damascena*, dark blue larkspur, Italian millet, panicum millet, maize tops and quaking grass (*Briza maxima*).

Creating a floral sheaf

To begin with, encase ordinary dried moss in chicken wire and mould it to the approximate shape of the head of the sheaf. (The use of wet fresh moss is not advisable as it would be likely to cause limpness and possibly rotting of the stems.) Attach a loop of double wire covered in florists' tape as a hanger.

Because it is not as easy to insert the stems into moss as into dry foam, trim all the stems short and wire them in groups using 90-gauge wire. Keep the off-cut stems and bind these separately. Wire the sunflowers individually with double wires. For added security (and to prevent scratching the wall), bend the wires that project through the back of the display round the chicken wire and return

the ends back into the moss. Use hot glue to fix some of the sunflowers and stalks in exactly the right places.

To establish the outline dimensions of the display secure into place several groups of stalks as well as some of the varieties forming the perimeter. It is important to make sure that all the flowers radiate from the same central point in the sheaf; an informal group of sunflowers is used here as a focus. Concentrate varieties with dense, circular flower forms – the *Centaurea, Echinops,* and *Helichrysum* – in this area too. Place *Nigella* (round in form but less strong in colour) further out, and make up the perimeter of the more directional, linear varieties – larkspur, maize tops, millet and quaking grass. Fill in the mass of lower stalks and trim them to length. For a clean effect the stalks would have to be stripped of leaves, but here a natural and informal look is required reflected by the mixture of leafy and slightly bent stalks.

The quotation in this instance was painted on to handmade paper made of banana fibre. The paper was then cut into strips and glued into place. (For a more rustic look, tie a simple bow of raffia or natural hessian around the sheaf.)

The quotation *'Floreat atque semper floreat'* is particularly appropriate for a collection of dried flowers. *Floreo* means 'flourish' or 'flower', so the meaning is simply 'Let it flourish and always flourish'. This is surely a fitting sentiment for flowers whose beauty can long outlive their natural life; which have given pleasure to people throughout history; and which show every sign of providing joy and inspiration into the future.

references

Culpepper's Complete Herbal (Wordsworth Editions, 1995)

A Modern Herbal Mrs M. Grieve (Tiger Books International, 1994)

Jekka's Complete Herb Book Jekka McVicar (Kyle Cathie, 1994)

Period Flowers Jane Newdick (Charles Letts & Co. Ltd., 1991)

The Complete Book of Everlastings Mark and Terry Silber (Alfred A. Knopf Inc., 1964)

Dried Flower Gardening Joanna Sheen and Caroline Alexander (Ward Lock, 1991)

All the dried flowers used in the book were supplied by The Hop Shop – Caroline Alexander's own specialist farm shop:

The Hop Shop
Castle Farm,
Shoreham,
Sevenoaks,
Kent TN14 7UB
United Kingdom

Tel: +44 1959 523219
Fax: +44 1959 524220
E-mail: hopshop@farmline.com
Web site: www.hopshop.co.uk

Mail order and trade enquiries are welcome. Tours of the flower fields and drying kilns can be booked in season.

acknowledgements

Sincere thanks to Kyle Cathie for providing such a superb production team – especially Sara Taylor, the photographer and Sophie Bessemer, the editor. They were a delight to work with and the book bears testament to their professionalism.

Special thanks to Laraine Doorey who assisted with the creation of some of the arrangements in this book.

My husband, William, has been a continuing inspiration, providing sound advice with unquenchable good humour.

photographic acknowledgements

All photographs by Sara Taylor except those credited below.

half-title: Geoff Hayes
11: Geoff Hayes
14: Mary Evans Picture Library
15: Electa Einaudi Mondadori
19: Rose: Gallica, red afficinal rose, illustration to 'A Collection of Roses' by Lawrence, 1799. Royal Botanical Gardens, Kew, UK/Bridgeman Art Library
20: Suttons Seeds
21: Lavender, Temple Bar, from 'Cries of London', pub. by Richard Phillips (1778–1851) 1804 (engraving) by William Marshall Craig (fl.1788–1828) Private Collection/Bridgeman Art Library
28: William Alexander
29: Jacqui Hurst
30: Sian Irvine
31: Sian Irvine
32: Sian Irvine
33: top left William Alexander, right Geoff Hayes
34: bottom left Sian Irvine, right William Alexander
35: William Alexander
36: Geoff Hayes
38: William Alexander
39: Sian Irvine
48: Jacqui Hurst
49: William Alexander
52: top left (3 photographs) William Alexander, centre right JS Sira/Garden Picture Library
53: top William Alexander, bottom William Alexander
54: Chris Burrows/Garden Picture Library

55: bottom left Mel Watson/Garden Picture Library, top right Geoff Hayes
56: bottom left William Alexander, top right William Alexander
57: bottom left John Glover/Garden Picture Library, top right William Alexander
58: bottom left William Alexander, top right Michael Howes/Garden Picture Library
60: bottom left William Alexander, top right Geoff Hayes
62: bottom left Clay Perry, top right Brian Carter/Garden Picture Library
63: bottom left William Alexander, top right William Alexander
65: top left William Alexander, bottom right Geoff Hayes
66: bottom Jerry Pavia/Garden Picture Library, top right Geoff Hayes
68: top William Alexander, bottom William Alexander
69: bottom left Lamontagne/Garden Picture Library, top right Geoff Hayes
70: top right Ron Evans/Garden Picture Library
71: bottom Karin Craddock/Garden Picture Library, top Geoff Hayes
73: Howard Rice/Garden Picture Library
74: bottom right Geoff Hayes
75: top left Geoff Hayes, bottom right Chris Burrows/GardenPicture Library
76: centre William Alexander, top right William Alexander
79: top Geoff Hayes, bottom William Alexander
154/155: Geoff Hayes

index